Handguns and Freedom

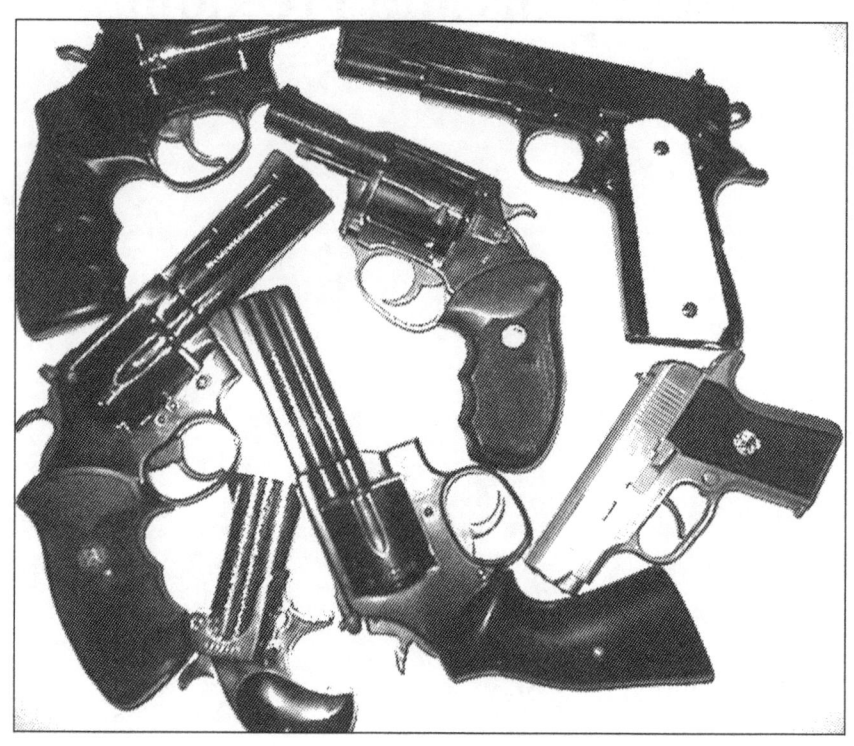

Some popular handguns used for self-defense in the United States.
From top left, clockwise: Taurus model 66, .357 magnum caliber, 2.5"
barrel; Springfield model 1911-A1, .45 ACP caliber; Colt "Pony", .380
ACP caliber; S&W model 586, .357 magnum caliber, 4" barrel; American Derringer "Lady Derringer", .38 Special caliber; Colt "Boa", .357
magnum caliber. Center: Charter Arms "Bulldog", .357 magnum caliber.

Handguns and Freedom

✦

...their care and maintenance

Joe Pierre

Writers Club Press
New York Lincoln Shanghai

Handguns and Freedom
...their care and maintenance

Writers Club Press
an imprint of iUniverse, Inc.

For information address:
iUniverse, Inc.
2021 Pine Lake Road, Suite 100
Lincoln, NE 68512
www.iuniverse.com

ISBN: 0-595-26056-X (pbk)
ISBN: 0-595-65511-4 (cloth)

Printed in the United States of America

Dedicated to all of the ardent defenders of the palladium of the Bill of Rights, the Second Amendment

Have no fear of any man
No matter what his size;
When danger threatens, call on me
And I will equalize.

—Verse packaged with early Colt revolvers

Contents

Acknowledgements

I would like to acknowledge all of my shooting instructors and companions, both in the U.S. Navy and in The Oregon Department of Corrections—too many to name here—as well as the invaluable friendship, training and advice of my great friend, the late George Lane Tooley, and the late Warden Hoyt Cupp. Also, I am grateful to all of the staunch people in the shooting community with whom I have shared so much pleasure during the years past.

Unless otherwise specified all of the photographs and artwork in this book are the work of the author.

Handguns And Freedom

Joe Pierre

Cover design and photograph by the author. 18-inch Bowie knife at bottom made by the author.

Foreword

I have been considering writing this book for some time now. There are, of course, many good books on the care and feeding of firearms—many of them on handguns—by some highly qualified people. Several of them are more qualified than I to write on the subject by virtue of their experience in the field of firearms training and long years of use in the military, law enforcement and competition.

Yet, I have some things to say that have not been said, perhaps, and that are worth expression. While I'm at it, I'll repeat some things that have been said because they bear repeating, and because some of my readers may not have read all of the other books on the subject.

This book is about privately owned firearms—particularly handguns—and freedom. In it I would like to clarify some common misconceptions concerning both the use and care of firearms and the natural right to self-defense, which is affirmed in our Constitution, in the Second Amendment.

Joe Pierre

Preface

My own experience in the field of firearms dates back over 60 years, when I was in my early 'teens. We were Westerners, and there were always firearms in the house. For the most part, they were rifles and shotguns, but we grew up with them. Like most Western households, we viewed them as tools—primarily for hunting meat. No one I knew hunted for trophies, although most households had an elk or deer's rack mounted on the garage—not the head, just the antlers.

On my seventeenth birthday, I joined the Navy. There, in San Diego, I learned to fieldstrip a .45 ACP caliber Colt semi-automatic pistol and shoot an M1 Garand semi-automatic rifle on a 600-yard range. Later I took instruction on, and fired .30 and .50 caliber machine guns.

While I was stationed at the Marine Corps Air Facility in Tsingtao, China, in 1948, I became familiar with the .45 caliber sub-machine gun known as the "grease-gun", and was also armed with .38-Special Smith & Wesson revolvers and Winchester model '97 pump-action shotguns, as well as the .45 ACP caliber Thompson sub-machine gun.

After retirement from the Navy, I joined the Oregon Department of Corrections, where I was required to qualify with a variety of rifles, pistols, shotguns and, again, the Thompson sub-machine gun.

While employed there I joined the pistol team at the Oregon State Correctional Institution, and at one point became a member of the Oregon Pistol Team—a 4-man team whose members are decided in statewide competition.

The result is that, at the age of 73 I have more than a speaking acquaintance with firearms, and particularly pistols since I have burned up thousands of rounds of ammunition with them. In the process of gaining the experience that I have with firearms, I have reached a few conclusions and formed some opinions about guns, and people, and the natural right to self-defense, which is the reason I am writing this book.

Joe Pierre

1

It's a Jungle Out There

I t's a jungle out there! I once wrote a letter to the editor of the local daily newspaper in which I stated that human beings were carnivores, and thus were by nature violent, since in their natural environment meat-eaters must first kill in order to eat. My point was that we must have laws, and abide by them, in order to live in peace with each other. We are a naturally violent species.

Of course another reader, of a more liberal persuasion than I, immediately protested that we were not carnivores, but omnivores, and thus we have a choice.

The word carne translates to meat. Omnivores eat meat. They also eat vegetation, but the more significant factor in this discussion is that they eat meat, and thus they are designed by nature to kill—a violent act.

We are primarily meat-eaters. As a species we get a large amount, if not most of our protein from eating flesh. In some places they eat much less meat than we do here in the United States—in the Orient, for example—but they do eat it as often as they can get it.

The fact that we buy our meat nicely shrink-wrapped in plastic at the supermarket does not change our basic nature. Our eyes give us away. We are hunters. Our eyes are placed in the front of our head, called binocular vision, rather than at the side, as are those of the grazers who must be aware of predators in their vicinity and thus have more peripheral vision.

We simply hire others to do our killing and butchering for us, just as we hire policemen to maintain law and order—another of our individual responsibilities. But if the two million year history of the human race were measured in feet and inches, and a mile represented our total history, only in the last couple of inches have we been so pampered. Our ancestors only a couple of generations back had to kill their meat. Genetically we are killers. Humans are violent creatures by nature. It is, indeed, a jungle out there—the main difference being that in the cities where most of the population lives we have tall buildings rather than tall trees.

And some of the denizens of our cities are violent, indeed. As I write this, a sniper, who is ruthlessly killing people apparently at random, for whatever motive, is terrorizing the Washington, D.C. area.

We are the dominant species on the planet, and we did not get in that position by default. No other species stands a chance against us except perhaps germs, microbes and viruses, and that only because we can't see them. Every indicator demonstrates our appetite for violence: the propensity for warfare, the brutality many members of our race show to weaker specimens, and the unnecessary acts of cruelty we read about every day in the newspaper. Even our games are predicated on warfare.

Each month the National Rifle Association, in their publications, run a monthly column entitled *The Armed Citizen,* in which they report up to a dozen or so cases where armed citizens defended themselves from violent aggressors with a firearm. They have run these stories for years, their source being the daily newspapers across the country.

The squeamish among us, and their numbers are legion—especially in our cities, it seems—often become ill at the sight of blood. The thought of killing a beef or pig, or wringing the neck of a chicken for their dinner makes them swoon. Many are so disturbed at the thought of eating flesh and the violence that must precede it that they become vegetarians. I sympathize with the latter, and honor them for their principles. Most who say, "I could never kill," simply buy their hamburger or fried chicken without giving a thought to the necessary action that put their meal before them.

When you are attacked, it is your natural right to defend yourself from your attacker—law or no law! Better to be tried by twelve than carried by six! If your attacker is the stronger, then, in self-defense—to prevent injury to yourself, you will try to equalize the contest with a club, knife, or other weapon. It is a natural reaction. No one willingly allows someone else to maim or kill him or her. The framers of the Constitution of the United States recognized that fact when they wrote the Bill of Rights, without which the Constitution would not have been ratified.

The framers of the Constitution did not grant us the right to bear arms in self-defense—they simply recognized it as a natural right and forbade the government to infringe on that right. It was a good idea, while it lasted. Unfortunately, over time our elected representatives in the Congress have sold us out, being more concerned with their own political future than the well being of their countrymen. Although sworn to uphold the Constitution of the United States—the instrument that created the federal government in the first place and granted it the powers that it enjoys, all carefully enumerated by the framers—they have forsworn themselves. They pass legislation regularly that is unconstitutional on its face, and create unconstitutional functions of government that would make the framers weep in despair—and they get away with it.

Now, today, there are over 20,000 laws in this country that regulate our right to keep and bear arms, in direct defiance of the proscription in the Bill of Rights.

There are a number of people in the Congress and among the media elite who have dedicated themselves to the destruction of the Second Amendment. They are almost entirely of the politically liberal persuasion, and many openly admit that their agenda is to totally disarm the people of the United States in direct contravention of the Bill of Rights. Members of Congress introduce bills to outlaw "cop-killer bullets," "assault rifles," "Saturday night specials," and magazines that hold more than ten rounds of ammunition. In addition, our former president forbade the import of semi-automatic firearms not significantly different than many of domestic manufacture. The liberal media elite back them up by broadcasting whatever figures they are fed, claiming such blatant lies and distorted facts about the "dangers" of private firearm ownership that the public, with little access to the actual figures and frequently having little or no experience of their own to draw from, often buy the propaganda.

The bullets designated "cop killers" were simply Teflon coated copper-plated handgun bullets. No policeman has ever been killed with such a round penetrating his body armor. The semi-automatic so-called "assault rifles" biggest fault is that they are ugly. They are made to look like military firearms, but functionally are no different than any other semi-auto. The Pentagon's Small Arms Identification Guide's definition of an assault rifle is a selective-fire military rifle, capable of firing on full automatic, burst, or semi-automatic at the option of the shooter.

A semi-automatic weapon fires one round with each pull of the trigger. So does an old-fashioned revolver like the .45 caliber Colt Single Action Army pictured below—introduced in 1873—or any other revolver. Functionally there is no difference. Semi-automatic firearms are as common as grass in the United States. A full-automatic weapon is a "machine gun." They fire continuously as long as the trigger is held down. It has required a special $200 license to own a machine gun in the United States since 1934, and such a legally owned firearm has never been used in the commission of a crime.

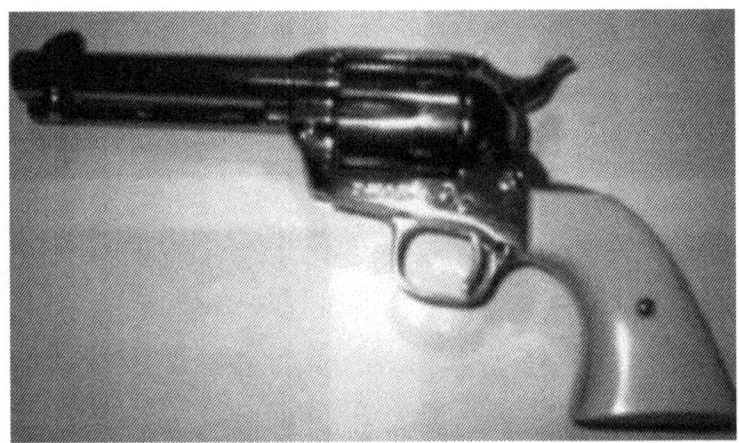

.45 Colt caliber Colt Single Action Army revolver

The so-called "Saturday Night Special," according to the gun-banners, is the weapon of choice of the criminal element. Nonsense! They are simply inexpensive firearms in small calibers. The very firearms that America's poor, among the most victimized by violent crime in our society, must depend upon for self-defense.

As for the criminals' "weapon of choice," they make their livings with their weapons. For the most part, they steal them, and they want large calibers and the best they can get. I know. I spent twenty years among them as a prison officer.

There are many cogent arguments and statistics that show the desirability of the private ownership of firearms: such ownership tends to reduce crime, and save lives. In fact, armed citizens help to rid the society of crime and contribute to law and order. The criminal element is far more concerned about the danger of getting shot than of going to jail.

The Second Amendment was not about duck hunting, or recreational shooting. It was about self-defense, and the people's last resort against tyranny by their own government, a situation that the framers of the Constitution recognized because they had just freed themselves from such a government.

There are those who argue against individually owned fire-arms—usually, however, they have armed protection available to themselves and their families.

2

Which Weapon is for You?

So, you have decided to buy a handgun to protect yourself and your family, but you don't know which one is appropriate. Let's talk about it.

First, there are two basic types of handgun, the semi-automatic, which might look like this.

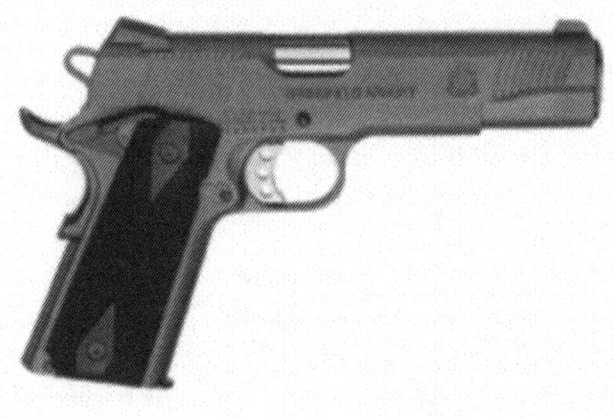

.45 caliber Springfield Model 1911-A1

Or perhaps you'd feel more comfortable with a revolver, which might look like this:

.357 magnum caliber Colt "Boa"

Of course, they make both types of firearm in many sizes and weights. Which one you choose will depend upon how you intend to use it—do you intend to carry it on your person, concealed, for example, or is it intended simply to stay in the home?—and on your level of experience with firearms.

For the beginner, I would recommend a revolver. The semi-automatic is a fine weapon. They automatically eject a spent round after it is fired, and immediately load another in its place ready to fire. Nothing else is required of the shooter than to pull the trigger, after the gun is armed—usually by pulling the slide back and then releasing it. Many people like semi-automatics for that reason, as well as for the fact that they carry, usually, more rounds of ammunition than a revolver and that reloading is usually faster. Most revolvers, in the larger calibers, carry only six rounds. Automatics may carry as many as ten in their magazine (which many erroneously call a "clip.")

What does a revolver do? Well, as a matter of fact it, too, fires every time you pull the trigger, just like the semi-auto. In addition, the semi-auto will sometimes jam—the most common type of jam being a "stovepipe" jam. A stovepipe jam is when a round that the slide picks up does not chamber, but instead stands straight up out of the receiver like a stovepipe. It is the easiest jam to clear, but it is still disconcerting—especially if you are in a desperate hurry to get a round off, as is the case in a rapid-fire competition or—more importantly—when your life is on the line.

Of course, it is possible that a revolver will jam, too, but that is more than likely the fault of the shooter not cleaning the gun properly, or the re-loader—probably also the shooter—not seating the primer properly in the cartridge. I would say that a revolver jamming is much less likely than the same phenomenon occurring in a semi-automatic. The revolver is sometimes referred to as "old reliable," because of its immediate availability and its reliability. For a beginner, then, I recommend the revolver. It requires less maintenance to keep it in working order, and there are no safety switches to remember and no slides to operate, to bring it into battery. All that is required is to aim it and pull the trigger.

We'll go into more detail on both types of firearms later. I usually carry a semi-automatic, since it is flatter and lends itself to concealed carry a little better. My personal choice is the .380 caliber Colt "Pony" double-action-only (DAO). It carries seven rounds, with one in the chamber, and fires just like a revolver without any safety to remember to release, nor the necessity to operate the slide to arm it. And, it weighs only 13 ounces!

I also have a revolver, which I sometimes carry. It is more powerful—a .357 magnum caliber—and it is only slightly heavier than the Colt. It carries only five rounds in the cylinder, however, and has a short barrel. It is a Charter Arms "Bulldog." You may view both of my carry guns in the frontispiece of this book.

I can carry either of them in holsters built into a T-shirt, under my shirt, or in an inside-the-pants holster which I bought from Dillon Precision in Arizona, the latter when I am wearing a sweater or an outside shirt or jacket and the former when I am lightly dressed with my shirt tucked into my trousers in warm weather, when a jacket or sweater is inappropriate. In either case, they are comfortable to wear and invisible to those around me.

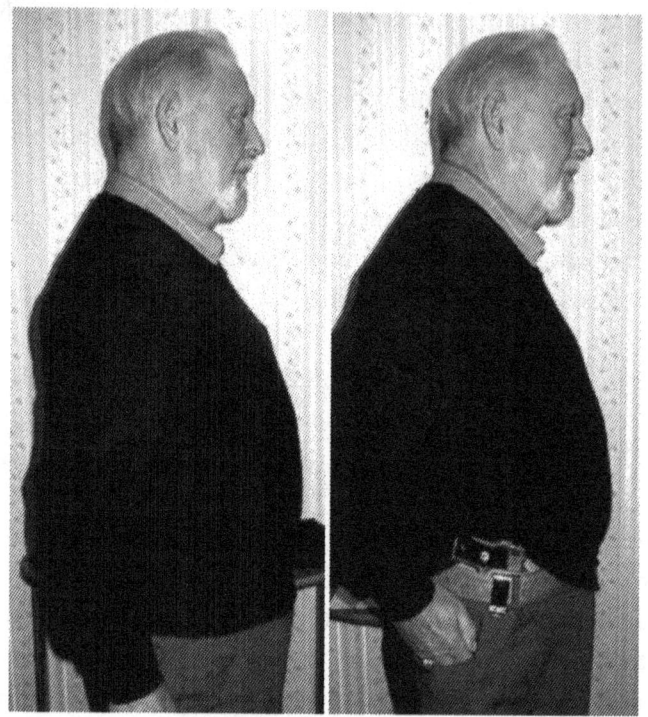

Carrying concealed with an inside-the-pants holster

Which brings up another sore subject. In Oregon, where I live, you may legally carry a firearm on your hip, in a holster clearly visible, without a permit of any kind. To carry a concealed weapon, however, it is necessary that you have a permit. The permits are expensive. Something like $100 at first, and then $50 for each four-year renewal.

I maintain that open carry of a weapon, whether it is a firearm or a large knife, can be seen as a threat. It certainly makes some members of the public uneasy, whereas carrying concealed bothers no one, since they are not aware that you are carrying a weapon. The politicians who dreamed up these laws have it exactly backwards!

In fact, since the Second Amendment states that the right of the people to keep and bear arms shall not be infringed, I think any laws restricting that right are clearly an infringement. Charging you money to exercise a right is certainly an infringement of that right, is it not?

But, the National Rifle Association has fought long and hard to get the states to pass "shall issue" laws, and so I paid for my license like everyone else.

So far thirty-two states have enacted "shall issue" laws (New Mexico being the most recent, in 2001). One state, Vermont, does not require a permit to carry a firearm, either concealed or openly.

So, what is a "shall issue" law? It is a set of requirements that a citizen must meet which, once met, require that they be issued a permit to carry a concealed weapon. The requirements vary with the state, but most often they include a clean record (no felony convictions, no drug history, no history of mental illness), fingerprinting, attendance in some kind of firearms training class, and the payment of a fee. The local authorities have no discretion. They may not deny a license to anyone meeting those requirements. Except for the fee, they are usually reasonable requirements. Seventeen states do not trust their citizens to be armed.

One should never trust a government that does not trust its citizens! In the United States, according to the Preamble to the Constitution, "We the people" are the power behind the Constitution, and therefore the power behind the government, which the Constitution created. At least, that is the way our nation's government was designed. It is supposed to derive its powers from the people, and only with their consent. Somewhere we have gone seriously astray!

Back to the subject of this chapter, which weapon should you buy? Again, if you are a beginner I would advise against purchasing a powerful caliber for your first handgun. The reason? Powerful calibers like the .357 magnum, or the .45 Automatic Colt Pistol (ACP)—especially in a light handgun with a short barrel—have a god-awful muzzle blast and recoil, and you need to work up to it gradually, gaining confidence as you go.

In the first place, when practicing with any firearm, in order to prevent damage to your eyes and ears, you should always use hearing and eye protection. Eye protection is usually accomplished with relatively ordinary looking glasses, except that many of them have a yellow tint to increase contrast. There are a variety of ear protection devices, ranging from simple earplugs to fancy electronic earmuffs that permit you to hear voices clearly—even slightly enhanced—but minimize the report of the firearm.

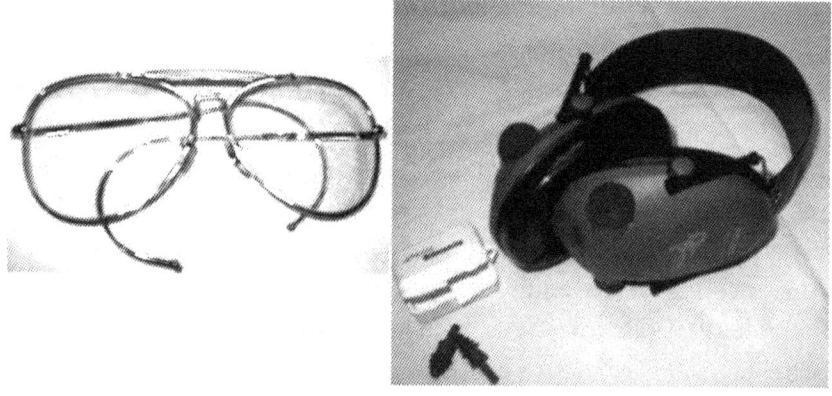

Use ear and eye protection when shooting

Of course, if you must use a firearm for protection, in a life and death situation, you will not be wearing eye and ear protection, but in such an event the rush of adrenalin in your system will likely prevent you from noticing such minor discomforts, and your life is more important than some damage to your ears.

As a matter of fact, in the military, back in the 'forties, we never used such amenities on the firing range. Whether they do today, I cannot say. Of course, many of my friends who used firearms a great deal in those early days have severe hearing loss today—those few who are still alive, that is.

The reason for the necessity of eye protection is the fact that, especially on a short range—twenty-five yards or less, which is typical of pistol ranges—there is some danger of ricochets from rock particles or lead, and the eyes are very vulnerable whereas a slight wound or scratch to other parts of the body might be relatively insignificant. Also, on rare occasions a hand-loader gets careless and overloads a cartridge, resulting in a blown up firearm. In such an event, not only the careless one, but also the fellow shooting at his side should be protected from flying particles. The chamber pressure in a firearm is great, and flying metal particles become shrapnel. It is only good sense to protect yourself from such eventualities. You will probably shoot for a lifetime without such an event spoiling your day, but we buy insurance against the possibility of an auto accident, although we hope it will never happen to us. Protect your eyes and ears.

To get back to the subject of which gun to buy, you might well start with a .357 magnum caliber, but only fire .38 Special cartridges in it. The .357 will fire both, and the .38 Special has relatively light recoil. It will also help if you purchase a moderately heavy revolver (the .357 magnum and .38 Special cartridges are revolver cartridges). Later, after you become accustomed to recoil, you can switch to the more powerful .357 magnum cartridge in the same gun. Many professionals practice with .38 Specials in their .357 magnum revolvers because it is more pleasant to shoot, and somewhat less expensive. A.38 Special fired from a .357 revolver with a 4-inch barrel, while wearing good ear protection, has minimal recoil and muzzle blast.

Even better, to begin with, is the humble .22 caliber pistol or revolver. It is an excellent way to develop a good trigger squeeze and sight picture. What you do *not* want is a light, short barreled .357 magnum as your first handgun. Even with good ear protection, it kicks like a mule. I have such a revolver, as I mentioned earlier, and I always practice with .38 Special cartridges. In fact, come to think of it, I always load it with .38 Specials even when carrying for self-protection. Here is the reason: the .357 magnum cartridge is very powerful, and it will penetrate most apartment walls with ease. The .38 Special, especially with a hollow-point or frangible bullet is not as likely to over penetrate. The other reason is that most self-defense shootings occur at very short range, and both the .38 Special and the .357 magnum, and for that matter even the humble .380 ACP have the same diameter bullets (.357 of an inch). There are differences of opinion, but for all practical purposes, if a .380 ACP won't do the job at a dozen feet distance, it is not likely that the .357 magnum will do much better even though it puts out a lot more energy.

People talk a lot about "mickey mouse" small caliber guns, like the .25 ACP and the various firearms chambered for the .22 long rifle cartridge—even the .32 ACP. They may not be the best choice for self-defense against a felon who is high on PCP and intent upon doing you bodily harm, but almost any of the experts would agree that they don't want to be shot with even a little .22 caliber firearm. As a general rule most agree that you want an authoritative caliber—as much gun as you can comfortably carry. Generally that means something of at least .32 ACP, and I feel better with a .38. It depends upon the circumstances. For example, if you are wearing a snug garment, or a tailored tuxedo, you might carry a tiny two shot .32 ACP Derringer in your pocket. I have one, and I have carried it in just such conditions. It's better than going "naked."

There is one important maxim: Never go to a gunfight armed only with a knife! The necessary caliber of the gun is open to discussion.

3

Some Inviolable Rules

Over the years, those who use firearms with any degree of regularity have developed some rules that everyone who has ever had any formal training with firearms has heard, and all but the most foolhardy would agree are the minimum requirements for safety. For your own protection and out of respect for those within range of your firearm, you should abide by them religiously. To fail to do so is not only insulting to your fellows, but it is downright criminal. If, as a result of your failure to conform to the rules you shoot someone, and they die as a result of your carelessness, you will probably be charged with negligent manslaughter or worse, and go to prison. Firearms are dangerous. They are designed to perforate the target. They are a useful tool for hunting, and they are a source of pleasure in sporting competition or simply for plinking at tin cans, but they can also be used for killing or injuring human beings.

There is a story going around about an old Texas Ranger: the Texas bureaucrats decided, in their wisdom, that the Rangers needed formal training with their firearms and ordered them to proceed to the range for instruction, in spite of the fact that the Rangers included some of the best pistol shots in the country.

Well, this old Ranger carried a .45 ACP caliber Colt Government Model 1911-A1 semi-automatic pistol, which is equipped with a grip squeeze safety. Because he had once been unable to fire his weapon in a life and death struggle with a felon, due to the fact that he could not adequately squeeze the grip, he subsequently applied a wet rawhide

16

strip around the grip, which when it dried put a permanent squeeze on the safety, rendering it useless for its intended purpose.

He was blessed with a gut that overhung his belt-buckle, but nevertheless wore his pistol tucked into the front of his trousers with the muzzle aimed squarely at his masculinity, but in a position that was most accessible in a pinch.

His instructor, when he saw the condition of the erstwhile safety device, and the way the Ranger wore his sidearm—but still respectful of the old Ranger—said, "Pardon me, Ranger, but isn't that dangerous?" To which the Ranger reportedly replied, "Son, if the danged old thang warn't dangerous, I wouldn't wear it!"

So, firearms are dangerous. In fact, they are potentially lethal. If they weren't, they would be useless as weapons. Always remember that.

So, here are the inviolable rules, which you must not only learn, but also practice, always:

Never assume a firearm is unloaded

Check it out yourself. In the case of a semi-automatic, it is not enough to drop the magazine. You must also visually and/or manually check the chamber and ascertain that there is no round in it.

When handing any handgun to another, in the case of a revolver, swing the cylinder out and hand it to them butt first.

In the case of a semi-automatic pistol, drop the magazine, rack the slide back and use the slide stop to lock it open. Then hand it to them butt first. Racking the slide back should eject any cartridge in the chamber, and they can visually inspect the open gun for themselves.

Handing the gun to another person

Never point a firearm at anyone

Never point a firearm at anyone or anything you don't want killed or damaged. Many innocent people have been killed and injured because someone pointed a firearm in their direction and pulled the trigger; usually in "fun." Being sorry doesn't bring the victim back to life. The same rule applies to furniture and other possessions that you would prefer to keep without holes in them.

Another thing: if you do intend to shoot, whether it is at a target in the woods, or an attacker intent upon killing or maiming you, you must consider what is behind your target. Remember that a bullet can penetrate the target and damage or kill whatever or whomever is behind it (remember what I said earlier about over penetration.)

There is even the remote chance you might miss, Heaven forbid.

In the movies you often see gunfights in crowded buildings or on a busy street. In real life no responsible citizen or law officer would ever engage in such an activity. Only a ruthless killer who doesn't care about anyone else would take such a chance.

Keep your finger off the trigger until ready to shoot

When you pick up a firearm or draw it from the holster, keep your finger outside the trigger guard. Too many people have shot themselves in the foot because of this common bad habit. They put their finger inside the trigger guard as soon as they touch the weapon.

On the firing range, the range officer will, or should, jump all over you if he observes you with your finger on the trigger at any time except when you are actually firing, and never, ever turn away from the target area holding your pistol aiming anywhere but down range. If you must engage in conversation, lay the pistol down and put the safety on. If it is a revolver, swing out the cylinder. Always remember that the tool you are holding is dangerous if handled improperly.

There are other safety considerations but those are the most important. Of course, gunpowder and alcohol are a bad combination!

The liberal press and the gun-banners would have you lock up your weapon and keep the ammunition in a separate secure place, to deny children or irresponsible people access to a loaded weapon, in the name of safety. It is certainly a good idea to keep the firearm away from the irresponsible; however, if you are keeping a weapon for self-protection it is useless if it is unloaded or inaccessible.

There are innumerable cases reported each year in the local press around the country (they usually go unreported in the national news) of "hot" burglaries, where the perpetrators break into a home violently and suddenly, counting on surprise and terror. Such attacks are without warning, and the victim has insufficient time to find and unlock their firearm, unlock the ammunition and load the weapon.

One way to keep it from children and the irresponsible is to carry it on your person. Another is to train your children to handle firearms safely.

These same people would have you rely on calling 911, rather than resort to self-defense, especially with a firearm. In most areas, if you have a burglary in process or are threatened by an enraged ex-husband or boy friend and you call 911, the police will arrive in twenty minutes or so, if they arrive at all. That is plenty of time for a murder, rape, or assault to occur and the perpetrator to vanish.

You are the only one who will always be present when danger threatens you. In the end, it is you who are responsible for your own safety. You cannot really count on anyone else to protect you and your family. Indeed, courts have repeatedly ruled that police are not responsible to protect the individual from harm. We hire them to catch the perpetrator after the crime has been committed.

Treat your firearm with the respect it deserves but remember, it will not fire itself. Due primarily to the safety classes held by National Rifle

Association instructors and others in the sport shooting community, the United States has the lowest accidental shooting rate in several decades—maybe ever—and not just per capita! The actual numbers of accidental shootings are at an all time low. But that is small comfort to the parent whose child has been shot accidentally.

Easy access to firearms is not the cause of gun deaths and injuries. Rather than accidental shootings, suicides and homicides account for almost all of them. As a matter of fact, Professor John R. Lott and David Mustard, in connection with the University of Chicago Law School, examined crime statistics for all counties in the United States from 1977 to 1992, and concluded that the thirty-one states allowing their residents to carry concealed weapons had significant reductions in their violent crime rates. They said that if those nineteen states that did *not* allow their citizens to carry concealed weapons had permitted them to, back then, their citizens would have been spared 1,570 murders, 4,177 rapes, 60,000 aggravated assaults and 12,000 robberies. In other words, they found that criminals respond rationally to deterrence threats. As I said earlier, they are more afraid of getting shot than they are of going to jail. In fact, most criminals realize the truth—that only a small percentage get caught by the police, and only a small percentage of *them* actually do time. Guns save lives.

Easy access these days is laughable, anyway. When I was in my forties, you could walk into any hardware store and most department stores in the country, excepting a few states, and buy a firearm—handgun, rifle or shotgun—pay your money and walk out with it. There was no federal form 4473 to fill out. You didn't even have to give your name.

In Oregon, in the small town in the tall timber country where my late wife lived, during hunting season the high school boys used to bring their hunting rifles and ammunition to school so that they could get an early start on the afternoon and evening hunt. And some of them, and their fathers, patrolled the Pacific coast beaches with their personally owned .30-30s or .30-'06s—watching for invaders, as volunteer coast-watchers.

That was in the early 1940s. Back then, virtually every household in the West kept guns. There was, indeed, easy access to firearms in those days—the very thing that the gun-banners and liberals decry today as the root cause of our violent society—blaming the tool, rather than the user. But in those days, there were no school shootings or drive-by shootings. We were at war, and Americans appreciated good marksmanship, and the President of the United States—a Democrat—praised the National Rifle Association for teaching it. There was no quibbling about the meaning of the Second Amendment Any politician who might have suggested then that it meant anything but what it said would have been tarred and feathered and run out of town on a rail.

How times have changed!

Now, a liberal political cartoonist publishes an inflammatory cartoon suggesting that the current sniper in the Washington, D.C. area is an NRA member! Our high schools forbid the government from recruiting for the armed forces on school property, and will not allow the Junior ROTC on campus. The pledge of allegiance is challenged because it contains the line, "under God." (That phrase was added only a few years ago—when I grew up we didn't use it.) And only a minority of the members of Congress has seen service in the uniform of their country.

But worse, we seem to have developed into a nation of children, who look to a paternalistic government to solve all of our problems, and seek security at the price of freedom. Security is a myth, and freedom, once lost will be long and costly to regain. When the world was in flames the people of other countries looked to the United States as their only hope to escape from tyranny. At great sacrifice this great country came to their aid, rescued them and helped them rebuild. If America trades freedom for the tyranny of socialism, who will there be to pull *our* fat out of the fire?

I friend sent this to me:

"How did our generation ever survive?

"Looking back, it's hard to believe that we have lived as long as we have.

"As children we would ride in cars with no seat belts or air bags. Riding in the back of a pickup truck on a warm day was always a special treat.

"Our baby cribs were painted with bright colored lead-based paint. We often chewed on the crib, ingesting the paint.

"We had no childproof lids on medicine bottles, doors, or cabinets, and when we rode our bikes we had no helmets.

"We drank water from the garden hose and not from a bottle.

"We would spend hours building our go-carts out of scraps and then ride down the hill, only to find out we forgot the brakes. After running into the bushes a few times we learned to solve the problem.

"We would leave home in the morning and play all day, as long as we were back when the streetlights came on. No one was able to reach us all day.

"We played dodge ball and sometimes the ball would really hurt.

"We ate cupcakes, bread and butter, and drank sugar soda, but we were never overweight; we were always outside playing.

"Little League had tryouts and not everyone made the team. Those who didn't had to learn to deal with disappointment.

"Some students weren't as smart as others so they failed a grade and were held back to repeat the same grade.

"Yet, our generation produced some of the greatest risk-takers and problem solvers. We had the freedom, failure, success and responsibility, and we learned how to deal with it all."

The ownership and use of a firearm carries with it the responsibility to learn to use it properly. Before you carry it for self-defense or depend upon it to protect your family, you should fire at least 100 rounds through it of the ammunition you will be using in it, without a problem, to insure its reliability. You should take instruction, if you are a beginner with firearms, from a competent instructor with the firearm you will be using.

You should invest a little time learning the laws of your state concerning the use of handguns, and when and where it is appropriate to carry them and fire them, and where and when it is not.

If you have a concealable handgun, in spite of the fact that I suggested a few pages back that such laws are unconstitutional, you should apply for and get a concealed weapons permit. The fact is that you usually can't win against the government. If, Heaven forbid, you ever have to use your weapon against an attacker, it will go far better for you if you are carrying it legally. In such an eventuality there is no doubt at all that you will end up in court in most venues—even if your action was legally justifiable. Even the worst crooks have friends who want their death or injury avenged and if you are not tried criminally, you will most likely be sued in civil court.

One other little thing: it is best never to make a comment to anyone about what you will do to someone if they attack you, such as "I'll blow their stinkin' head off!" If you ever do have to resort to a firearm to save your neck, such a statement can come back to haunt you, in court.

It is wise to avoid the places where violence is likely to occur: certain areas of town, and the watering holes to which the police are frequently called. You know the places. Give them a wide berth. If you are carrying a firearm, be very slow to take offense. Stay out of heated arguments. Listen quickly, and speak slowly.

Be careful out there.

4

The Fundamentals of Good Shooting

The basics of good handgun shooting involves five things, in the following order:

1. Trigger control

2. Sight alignment

3. Grip

4. Stance

5. Breath control

Trigger control is most important. If you're doing everything else right, but in that final split second you jerk the trigger, the bullet will end up in the north forty instead of in the black of the bullseye where you intended it to go.

There are two methods of shooting with most modern revolvers and semi-automatics: single action and double action. In the single action mode, you must first cock the weapon by thumbing the hammer back. In that mode the trigger pull required is usually quite light—as light as 2.5 pounds of finger pressure in some target pistols. In a weapon, it should be at least three pounds, and four is more conservative. This is the reason: if you are holding someone prisoner at gunpoint until the police arrive, with a light trigger pull you could easily shoot them unintentionally.

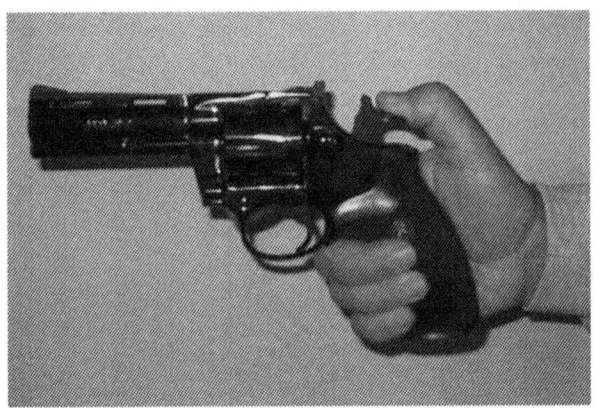

Thumb cocking a .357 magnum caliber Colt "Boa"

With a target gun's light trigger you can almost think a shot away. A light touch with your finger can touch off a round. A weapon is typically used when adrenaline is running high, and a more conservative trigger is called for.

The double action mode, on the other hand, enables the shooter to "trigger cock" the weapon. In other words, you pull back on the trigger and the hammer comes back to a point where the sear trips, and the pistol or revolver is fired. A much longer and harder pull is required; when I bought my Colt "Pony" double-action-only (DAO) semi-automatic for example, it had, as I recall, a 20 pound trigger pull. That is a hard pull. I had a different trigger spring installed and a trigger job done on it by a gunsmith, which reduced it to an eight-pound pull. That was much more acceptable. It is harder to hold a good sight picture with a very hard trigger. Of course, you must realize that if you lighten the trigger too much, the firing pin might be affected and the gun could be less reliable.

Back to trigger control—with a weapon you will, and should, use the double action method exclusively. For reasons best understood by the courts, it is considered reprehensible to cock the weapon with the thumb before firing it, although that method usually results in greater accuracy. It has to do with premeditation, which damages your case for self-defense. Lawyers like to pick on minor nuances to make their case.

For an education in the legal aspects of using a handgun for self-defense, you could do a lot worse than to read Massad Ayoob's various books on the subject. An experienced police officer, he often serves as an expert witness in such cases, almost always for the defense.

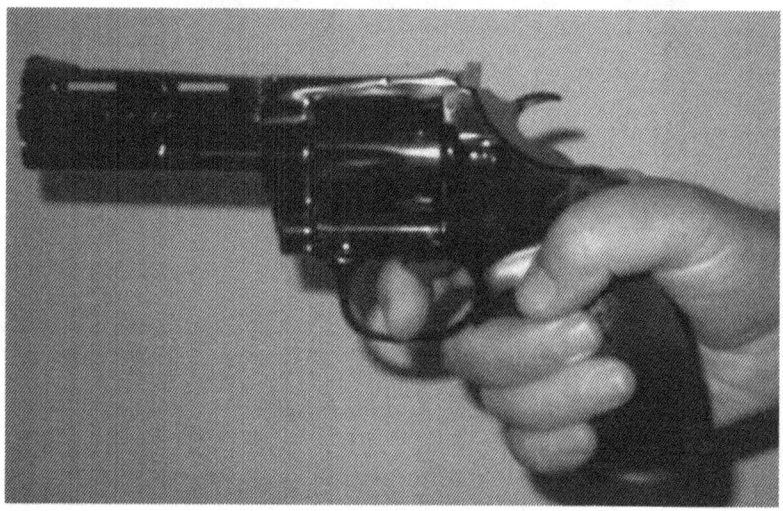

Trigger cocking a .357 magnum caliber Colt "Boa"

So, you will be trigger cocking your weapon, even if it has a hammer. Squeeze the trigger straight back deliberately without moving the front sight. Since you should be concentrating on lining up your rear and front sights with the target, you will not be able to watch the hammer come back, but if you could it would be deliberate and steady. Some say that the report, when the gun fires, should surprise you, but any regular shooter, after a few hundred rounds through the same weapon, knows exactly when the gun will fire. The point is that when it fires, the muzzle should not move perceptibly.

When shooting double action (trigger cocking) use the first joint of your trigger finger. You can apply more pressure without straining, which causes a shake, resulting in unnecessary movement.

When shooting single action (thumb cocking and then squeezing the trigger to let the round off), use the pad of your finger between the tip and the first joint. It is more sensitive, and not so much force is required.

In both cases, pull the trigger straight back in a deliberate manner without moving the muzzle either up and down, or sideways. Practice, practice, practice. Don't try for speed, either in drawing your weapon, or in firing. Speed, if it is ever necessary, will come naturally with time and practice. The main thing is to develop good habits. In a tight spot, after hours of practice (which can be fun in itself) you will find that the practiced methods will come back to you automatically.

The old "quick draw" stuff that Hollywood loves so well never really existed in the old West, anyway. One of the best-known killers, John Wesley Hardin, carried his revolver in a coat pocket lined with leather, instead of the much-loved low-slung holster. Most of the tales of Billy the Kid, Hardin and the rest are the result of the fevered minds of Eastern pulp authors and modern day Hollywood writers. Neither William Bonney (Billy the Kid) nor Hardin were killed in a shootout. Billy was ambushed in a dark room and Hardin was shot in the back.

My step-Granddad was a lawman in the Indian Territory (sometimes called "the Nations") before it became Oklahoma. I knew the old man well. He had cataracts on both eyes, resulting in very blurred vision. He ate every meal with only a hunting knife. He was a big, tough old man with a white handlebar mustache. I watched as my Dad threw a tin can in the air. Old Al deliberately unholstered his gun and kept the can bouncing in mid-air until his ammunition was exhausted.

He was not shooting a Colt Single Action Army revolver, as they all do in the movies. He was shooting a .30 caliber Luger semi-automatic pistol with a four-inch barrel, which he'd owned since around 1900. He was a real Westerner.

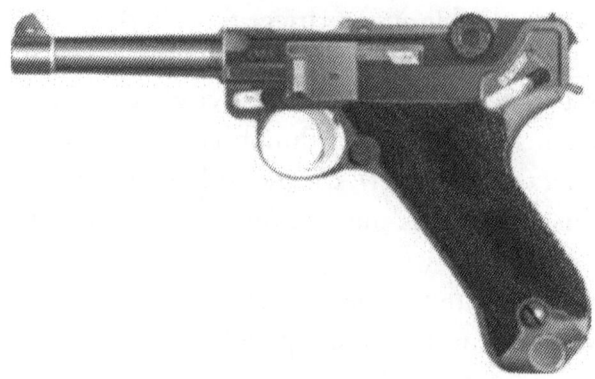

.30 caliber Luger semi-automatic pistol

Sight Alignment is next in importance to trigger control for achieving accuracy. If you are accurate with your first shot it will not be so important to have a firearm with a high capacity magazine. You will not have to "spray and pray" to incapacitate your attacker.

This is what your sight picture should look like when you are shooting at a bullseye target:

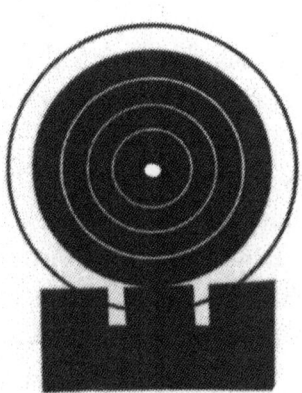

The front blade sight should be exactly centered in the notch of the rear sight and the top plane of both sights should be even, with the same amount of daylight on each side of the front blade, as shown. The lower limb (bottom) of the black circle should just kiss the top of the sight plane. This is called the "six-o'clock hold" because the center of the front sight is at the six o'clock position on the black of the target, if it were a clock face. If your firearm has adjustable sights, which are desirable for a target pistol, they should be adjusted so that the round "prints" (or ends up) in the center of the ten ring on the target as shown by the centered white dot above.

To adjust your sights, if they are of the adjustable type, remember to move the rear sight in the same direction you wish the point of impact of the bullet to move. In other words, if you wish the bullet to strike more to the right, move the rear sight to the right, and vice versa. If you wish the bullet to strike higher, adjust the rear sight upward. Most front sights are not adjustable, but if you must drift them, they move just the opposite of the rear sight.

Before and after you adjust them, fire several shots from a stable rest without any movement of the muzzle between shots. In other words, make sure that sight adjustment is necessary, and that it has accomplished what you set out to do.

At this point I want to emphasize that the six o'clock hold is appropriate for target practice; for a weapon intended for self-defense or to be used in battle it should be sighted "dead on" at some particular distance—this is primarily true of the rifle because ranges are longer. However, it is all right to sight your defensive weapon for a six o'clock hold for the 50 feet or 25 yards of the pistol target range, since it will be accurate enough at the extremely short range of most defensive shooting where you will simply point and shoot.

There is little point in sighting your handgun for 100 yards, when in all likelihood it will be used at a range of a dozen feet for defensive use or on a target range. Indoors pistol target ranges are likely to be 50 feet, and outdoors typically 25 yards. Also, for a strictly self-defense weapon it is just as well to have a pistol or revolver with fixed sights, or in some cases no sights at all. They are less likely to be knocked out of alignment. The fixed sights are usually dovetailed into the pistol or revolver, and thus can be adjusted by drifting, at least for windage (side-to-side adjustment) though not for elevation except perhaps to file one or the other down a bit.

There is another thing that you will find out for yourself very quickly: you will not be able to get a crisp, sharp view of the rear sight, front sight, and the target at the same time. Your eyes will only focus sharply on one plane at a time. So, you concentrate on the front sight. The rear sight and the target will be somewhat blurred. That's okay. A little practice will confirm that you can shoot very accurately in spite of the fuzziness.

In the pistol matches I used to attend, the ten ring of the slow fire fifty-foot target was about the size of a nickel. Yet, my shooting partner on the Oregon Correctional Institution Pistol Team, Captain Hoyt Cupp, and I used to routinely shoot in the mid to high nineties. He was the better shot. That is, we managed to hit or cut the ten ring on an average of nine out of ten times at fifty feet. We both had very good target pistols and were shooting .22-caliber standard velocity Remington "green box" ammunition, which in those days was the good stuff. I used an S&W model 41 with specially made grips, and he fired a Hi-Standard "Supermatic" Citation, one of the best target pistols around (no longer in production. Like many other fine gun manufacturers Hi-Standard succumbed to the political and market pressures of the last few years.)

Another problem that makes accurate pistol shooting more difficult than shooting a rifle well—you will discover that your pistol tends to wobble back and forth and up and down across the target. This is normal. There is a secret to trigger control that Captain Cupp taught me to obviate the problem. It is simple, and it truly helps: squeeze the trigger when you are on target and hold up when you drift off. "Squeeze when you're on, hold up when you're off!"

Below are some pictures that should be self explanatory of what happens with various sight pictures. They are exaggerated in order to make the point.

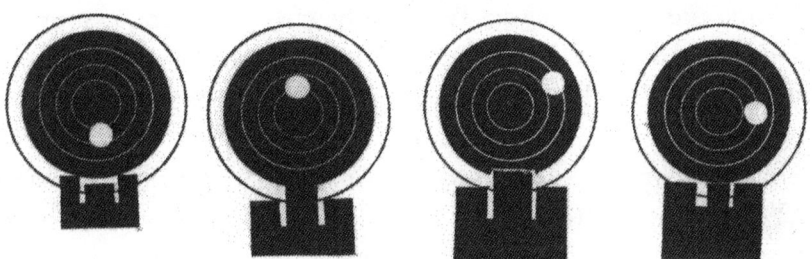

Front blade down, shot low. Front blade up, shot high. Front blade to left or right, shot left or right respectively.

Jerking the trigger can also send the shot left, if it stays on the paper at all. Any movement of the muzzle while getting the shot off will of course result in inaccuracy. Short barrels are most difficult.

Have you noticed how the movies lately show the shooter holding his handgun canted to the left? Often the left side of the pistol is parallel to the ground! Needless to say, that is a stupid way to hold a firearm, and inherently inaccurate.

I've always thought it strange that so many of the entertainment icons—Oprah, Rosie, Barbra, and others—none of whom know anything about firearms except that they are against them, are sustained by an industry that in one breath belittles the "gun-culture," and in the next produces movies that feature firearms and violence in every scene, with multiple gun battles, explosions and graphic scenes of violent death and language that would make a longshoreman blush.

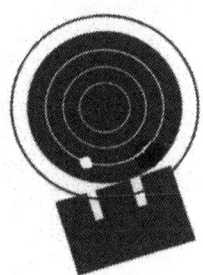

Holding the pistol sideways is probably where the phrase "spray and pray" originated. Those who use it in real life, if any, probably do it because it looks "kewl." Certainly not because it helps their score.

Using the correct grip is important because it contributes to accuracy. You should try to always hold the firearm as closely as possible exactly the same each time, and there is a right way and a wrong way. The handmade grip that I had on my target pistol was so closely fitted that I had to hold the gun the same way each time I picked it up. The pictures below demonstrate two ways of gripping a revolver—a right way and a wrong way. The same basic grip applies to the semi-automatic as well. Hold it with your hand high on the backstrap, like this:

Not like this:

Your grip on your firearm should be firm, but not so hard that it causes muscle fatigue. The same principles apply to a revolver as to an automatic pistol. With a revolver your hand should be high on the backstrap as shown in the above picture. On modern double-action revolvers there is a hump at the top of the backstrap. It should ride on top of your hand.

.45 ACP caliber Springfield 1911-A1

Most semi-automatics have a spur at the top of the backstrap that looks like the one on the pistol above. It serves the same purpose as the hump at the top of the backstrap on a double-action revolver. Your hand should ride high. Remember to keep your finger out of the trigger guard until you are ready to fire.

When you buy a pistol or revolver, you should check it out and make sure that it fits your hand. A woman with small hands will be unhappy with a large pistol, which she cannot hold properly. A person with large hands will have a hard time with a tiny pistol. Sometimes an aftermarket grip will solve the problem, but no grip will fit everyone. Earlier I mentioned that on my target .22 I had special grips made to fit my hand exactly. I traced around my hand and sent the drawing to the grip maker in Lewiston, Idaho. It was virtually impossible to hold the grip on that pistol in anything but the correct way. It fit like a glove, and contributed to my good scores.

Speaking of weapons that could make a woman unhappy, see the following photo:

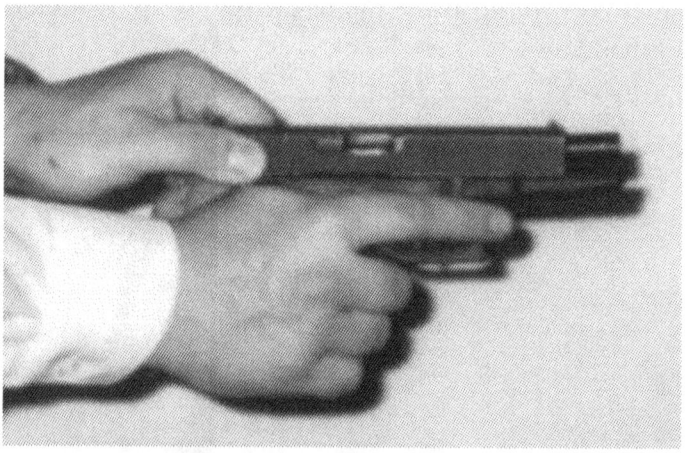

In order to arm most semi-automatic pistols (take a round from the magazine and inject it into the chamber where it is ready to fire), it is necessary to rack the slide back and release it. On some firearms the slide is very stiff and resists the action, so that some hand strength is required. Some ladies find this extremely difficult to accomplish (some men, also). For that reason, it is wise to try the action before you buy, and keep shopping if the action is too stiff—perhaps you should go to a revolver, instead of an automatic.

I would like to stress again that functionally the modern double-action revolver is just as good as the semi-automatic with certain reservations. It carries only six rounds in the cylinder in the larger calibers, usually. There are a couple of exceptions. It is arguably slower to reload, although some have developed great skill in that department and can actually reload at about the same speed as an automatic, especially with a speed-loader.

It fires with every pull of the trigger, just like a semi-auto, and in addition if there should be a misfire (a cartridge, for whatever reason, fails to fire when the firing pin strikes the primer)—often because the primer has been subjected to oil during the cleaning process—the revolver shooter can simply pull the trigger again, which brings another cartridge into battery and fires it. The semi-auto requires that the slide be manually racked back, which ejects the spent cartridge and carries another round into the chamber.

The stance of the shooter is the next in importance for accurate shooting. It is directly related to type of shooting you are doing, and also influences your grip on the firearm. If you are shooting in 3-gun competition at bullseye targets, you will stand like this, with your feet at a 45 degree angle to the target and one arm sticking out full length, with the other hand in your pocket:

In case you wondered, the three guns in such competition are the .22 caliber semi-auto mentioned previously, the .45 caliber pistol or revolver (mine was a Colt "Gold-Cup" National Match model) and any center fire handgun .32 caliber or over. In the '60s many of us used revolvers. Mine was a Colt Officer's model with a bull barrel—the forerunner to the famous Python, but in .38 Special caliber.

In those days, everyone shot one-handed. More recently some other techniques have developed, which offer a steadier gun platform. One such is the Weaver stance, pictured below:

Another result is a change from the one-handed grip to the two-handed, with some variations. But the stance is radically different. The bird's eye view, below, shows the difference in the position of the feet for the two-handed position, as well as two dissimilar stances for one-handed shooting. There are variations to all of them, for example, the Weaver stance, above, uses a crouched position.

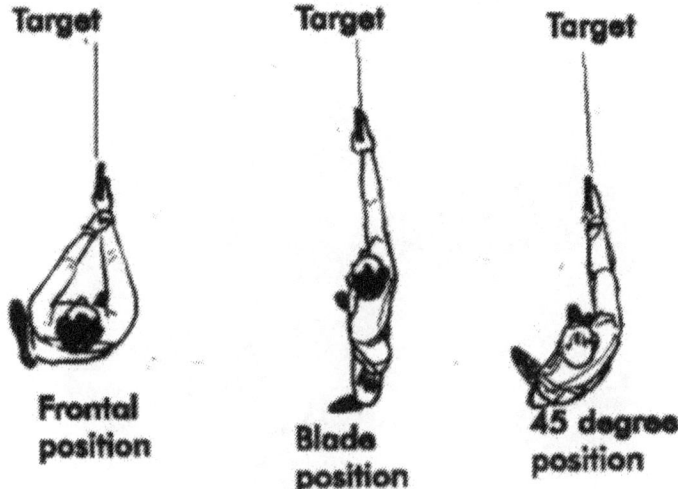

Of the two one-handed positions, the blade position does not give adequate resistance to windage (sideways movement in a wind), and the frontal position would be less than ideal for shooting one-handed, so a compromise is called for: the 45 degree position.

Shooting two-handed, the stance and grip are adapted for the greatest stability, and this is the method that has been adopted by most professionals—police, military, and action shooters who compete in IPSC and USPSA matches.

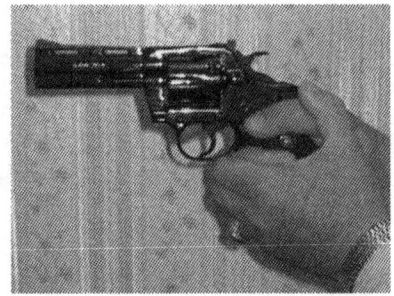

Above is the stance and grip used most often. There are variations in the grip, as I stated earlier. For strengthening the wrist, it might look like this:

One should use the stance and grip that is most natural and comfortable and gives the most accurate result. The ones shown above, however, have been adopted by some of the best shooters in the country. It is not necessary to re-invent the wheel.

Breath control is the last and least important of the elements that contribute to accurate shooting. Of course while one is triggering a round off it is desirable to hold the firearm as steadily as possible, so you want to avoid movement. The most important of all the elements contributing to accurate shooting, as I said before, is trigger control. If you jerk the trigger, the muzzle will move at precisely the wrong moment and the shot will certainly go astray. If you have a poor sight alignment, the bullet will not strike precisely where you want it to, but if trigger control is good, you'll at least be in the ballpark. Grip is important, but holding the gun unwaveringly when the bullet exits the muzzle is far more important, providing that the pistol is pointed in the right direction. Also, grip is important in getting back on target immediately in case you need to get off that second shot. Stance assists to the same end.

There is another reason why breath control is less important—if you have been running and you are breathing hard, you will need to get hold of yourself and try to calm down before you touch of a shot, otherwise you won't be able to hold a sight picture and the firearm will be jumping up and down in your hand with each breath; but in ordinary every day target shooting, you will normally hold your breath without even being aware of it. On the range, everyone I have ever watched shoot has held his or her breath automatically. It is just basic human nature to do so when you are concentrating on your sight picture and controlling your trigger squeeze.

In target shooting, slow fire is the toughest because the 10-ring is so small, and your concentration must be at a high level, and you have lots of time to get off your shots. Most shooters shoot and then drop the muzzle to the table in front of them, maybe check the shot in their shooting scope, and raise the pistol for another shot. Trying for perfection, they sometimes hold the sight picture and their breath too long, "squeeze when you're on, hold up when you're off!" After a few moments, the wobble gets worse. Take your finger off the trigger, lower the muzzle, and give it a rest. Then try again.

Timed and rapid fire are easier: the 10-ring is huge compared to slow fire. You have twenty seconds to get off five rounds in timed fire and ten seconds for a five-shot string in rapid fire. Lots of time. Those are the times in an NRA sanctioned match. Olympic matches cut the time—in rapid fire you only have five seconds for five rounds. Still, it is not spray and pray. You have plenty of time to aim each round.

Shooting a firearm without first aiming is a fool's game. That is not to say that you should never simply point the firearm; even from the waist pointing is aiming, but it takes considerable practice. When you point your finger you are aiming at something. Aiming a pistol is a similar task.

5

The Practice of Shooting

Like any other activity that demands a level of skill—golf, horseshoes, driving a vehicle, casting with a fly rod—you get better with practice, and in order to keep your skill level you must practice regularly.

Also, like most other activities you should avoid practicing bad habits, as they will become ingrained and more difficult to lose when you realize that they *are* bad habits. It is well to have a competent instructor in the beginning. The self-taught practitioner usually reflects on his teacher's lack of qualification.

The following are some of the bad habits that many self-taught shooters get into. Some are easily overcome, and some are more difficult.

One of the common problems is simply how you begin to address the target with your firearm—many shooters raise their pistol above eye level, and then bring it back down until it bears on the target. That is wasted time and motion. In many Western movies you see the hero raise his weapon, point it at the sky, and then try to throw the bullet at the target. Absolutely ridiculous! Simply raise it to eye level, align the sights and fire. You can't help the bullet to the target by throwing it. When you raise the barrel above eye-level, you must simply lower it again to reach the position again that you have already passed.

If, after extended shooting, your arm begins to tire or shake with fatigue, lower your weapon to the table (if you are on the range) and shake out the cramp, or flex your fingers. Your final score will be better than if you try to "get it over with" and keep shooting. Reach over with your weak hand, put your weak hand thumb under the hammer, pull the trigger and let the hammer down gently with your thumb. If your firearm is equipped with a hammer block or transfer bar, as almost all modern revolvers are, there is no danger that it will fire after you release the trigger. Never leave a handgun loaded and cocked on the table, or anywhere else, unattended!

Dry firing is good practice for improving your trigger pull. One way to do it most effectively is to do it in front of a mirror. First, obviously, make certain that the weapon is not loaded; then aim at your reflection in the mirror, using the stance and grip that you have decided on based on the information in the last chapter, or your instructor's suggestions. You might aim at your eye in the mirror. Get a perfect sight picture and practice your trigger squeeze, making it slow and deliberate. If, when the trigger lets off, there is any muzzle motion you will see it clearly.

If you practice faithfully on a regular basis, then when the moment comes and the adrenalin is pumping and your heart is beating so hard you will be sure everyone will hear it, your practice sessions will pay off. You'll do the right thing automatically.

Practicing on the range, have your shooting partner load your revolver (this won't work with a semi auto) and leave one or two chambers empty. If you are anticipating your shot and flinch, it will show dramatically when you click on the empty chamber unexpectedly

Flinching is a common problem, and it can be overcome only with good, regular, consistent practice. The two methods described above are probably the best antidotes. The cause of the flinch is usually simply exposure to firing a weapon with heavy muzzle blast and recoil, often exacerbated by not wearing hearing protection. Almost every shooter experiences it at some point. Anticipating the shot is the major cause. You know the recoil and muzzle blast is coming, and from long practice, you have learned the exact point in the trigger pull when it will occur. You must concentrate on the slow deliberate pull and on the sight picture without wavering. Keep your mind on those two things, and the flinch will disappear.

Call your shots. As you fire in practice, get in the habit of calling your shots, even silently, to yourself if you don't have a shooting buddy (it is always better to shoot with someone else—especially in the wilderness, rock quarry, or other places where you will be alone away from help in case of an accident). Imagine the target as the face of a clock, and as you fire, judging from your sight picture and any muzzle movement at the time the gun went off, say to yourself, silently or aloud, "Six o'clock, high," or "three o'clock, low," according to your feeling about the shot. Then, if you have a spotting scope, which most serious shooters sooner or later acquire, check out the shot on the target to see how accurate you were with your call. With practice, you will eventually become quite accurate, and it will also help you to develop trigger control and a better sight picture.

Tasco 18-36 power Spotting Scope

If you are really serious and get into competitive bullseye shooting, you will no doubt eventually procure a shooting box.

Shooting box

I procured this one from Champion Shooting Supplies. It will hold four pistols, as well as ammunition, cleaning supplies, targets, shooting glasses, earmuffs, and the spotting scope mounts on the lid as shown, which swings up.

There are any number of shooting accessories available for the person who gets into the sport seriously. Competitive shooting can be as expensive as you want, or as inexpensive as the cost of an NRA membership (for sanctioned matches), and the pistols and ammunition required for the match. Whether you have a small or large budget, you will probably get a great deal of enjoyment from the hobby.

Here, however, we are primarily concerned with the self-defense aspect of firearms. Skills learned in competition will certainly carry over to self-defense, but like any necessary insurance policy, there is a cost involved. The chances are good, depending upon where you live, that you will never have to use a firearm for self-defense in your lifetime, but don't count on it. You don't expect an auto accident when you buy auto insurance, either, but prudence dictates that you cover yourself. Usually there is a legal requirement, also, that you have insurance on your car—to protect others from loss as well as yourself and your passengers. Going armed serves exactly the same purpose. For example, if at several of the school shootings, and at Luby's Cafeteria, there had been an armed citizen present, the outcome would almost certainly have been different. Or, if there had been an armed citizen aboard one of the hijacked aircraft that hit the twin towers and the Pentagon, perhaps we could have averted the great loss of life. Instead of locking the barn door after the horse is stolen—coming up with new, more strenuous security measures at the airports which are only being observed on a hit-or-miss basis anyway—maybe we should do a 180 degree turnaround, and allow any passenger who has a concealed firearm to board. Forget the Air Marshals! Allow the pilots to be armed, as well as the passengers. The good guys always outnumber the bad guys, who would almost surely hesitate to start something if they thought they would not only fail in their mission, but also get shot.

Not long ago a British television crew interviewed me for a pilot show they hoped to air on BBC, called "Are We There Yet." They said up front that they were interested in me because of my pro-gun reputation. I agreed to the interview provided that they would not make it an anti-gun tirade, as television so often does. They assured me that it would not be. They sent me a tape of the final program after the interview, which included a fellow who claimed to have seen "Bigfoot," and footage of a hippy commune in the state, as well as some other American oddballs. It was clear that the program was to be about American weirdos. They treated all of them with great respect and credence in their post-mortems—except me, that is.

During the interview, they wanted to see my guns, of course, and to hear my views. I went out of my way to present a reasonable, well-dressed image of an American who respected the entire Bill of Rights, and I pointed out that it is that document which sets the United States apart from all other nations. One of their final questions was what I thought should be done about the school shootings in the United States. I pointed out that out of a 285 million population, one has to expect a few oddballs, and that the percentage would be insignificant were it not for the gravity of the crime.

I suggested that one solution might be to train some teachers in the handling of firearms and allow them to carry concealed firearms at school.

The remarks on the tape *after they left and were driving away* and I had no chance to respond were out of character from their demeanor during the interview, in which they presented themselves as friendly questioners. One of the female interviewers, who was American by birth and married to her producer who operated the camera, asked her girlfriend, who was from Seattle, what she thought of me. The friend answered, "I think he's a nice man, I think he's charismatic, I think he's intelligent, I think he's delusional—y'know he kinda had me goin' with him, I was gonna buy a lot of it, I was gonna allow him to peddle it and not get angry, and then y'know when we got inta the thing about the schools and make sure that our teachers have guns, my jaw just hit the floor! How incredibly ridiculous! I mean, you can't even spank a kid in school anymore and he's talking about giving the teacher a gun; I mean we don't even want to stop a child with corporal punishment, we just want to kill them!"

Of course, I said nothing of the sort. They asked me about the school-shooting problem. There would *be* no "problem" if students were not being killed. When a teenager has a gun and starts shooting people as fast as he can, then it is no longer appropriate to treat him as a "child." He is a killer. He forfeits the prerogatives of childhood. Besides which, in the one case I know of where an armed teacher stopped such an escapade, he didn't shoot the kid, he simply threatened him, and that was enough.

The same interviewer made a remark earlier in the show, which indicated her liberal political stance. Had I known of it before the interview, I would probably have refused to do it. They were watching the inauguration of President Bush on television, and she grimaced. Then she remarked that during the motorcade "*Nobody* was on the street, and I'm sure that half the country is *pissed off.*"

Certainly not all of the pro-civil-rights politicians are political conservatives—many stalwart defenders of the Second Amendment are Democrats who are truly trying to represent their constituencies and protect the Constitution, as they took a solemn oath to do—but most of the anti-gunners, whose dearest wish is to see the Second Amendment nullified, are from the politically liberal persuasion. There are a few Republicans, as well—mainly those who represent large urban areas—who are anti-gunners. I have often wondered what it is that makes the great majority of people who live in the heavily populated urban areas politically liberal, and those who live in the small towns and rural areas almost universally politically conservative. My best guess is that it has to do with self-sufficiency, as opposed to being dependent. The people who live in the cities are probably mainly paper-pushers and dependent on others for everything they eat and wear. Probably rural people feel less dependent simply because they produce the food and lumber and other essentials that the city folks depend on. In any case, it is surely a fact that the large urban areas are the center of the liberal political philosophy, and they almost universally are against private firearms ownership.

One of the reasons that city people have an inordinate fear of guns—I've seen them come into a room with a firearm in it and react as if they'd seen a cobra—is because they are unfamiliar with them, and also because cities like New York, Chicago and Washington, D.C., virtually ban them, and as a result muggings and shootings are endemic. There is far more violence in the large urban sprawls than in the less populated areas of the country, and it is easy for the gun-haters to persuade people who live in fear that the cause is "easy availability" of firearms. Gun laws are a cheap palliative. It is far easier for a politician to get another gun ban passed than to address the real causes of violence in a sick society. Take another gun law, and come back in the morning.

6

About Some Individual Firearms

L et's examine some individual firearms and see what makes them tick. They are truly remarkable instruments, when you think about it. They routinely handle chamber pressures up to 50,000 pounds per square inch or more, and the machine tolerances to which they are made are often remarkable. Take the Smith & Wesson model 586, for example:

An amazing piece of equipment; I purchased mine several years ago for under $350, and have found it to be utterly reliable and one of the most accurate handguns in my inventory. It is stock except for the grips, which I made myself of ebony. The price of a new model 686 (stainless steel—mine is blued steel) today is about double what it was twenty years ago, when I purchased mine. Guns are often very good investments, as well as useful tools.

Next we'll look at one of S&W's semi-automatic pistols. They make some of the best in the world. The name is familiar in virtually every country on earth; even those who do not speak English recognize the words "Smith & Wesson."

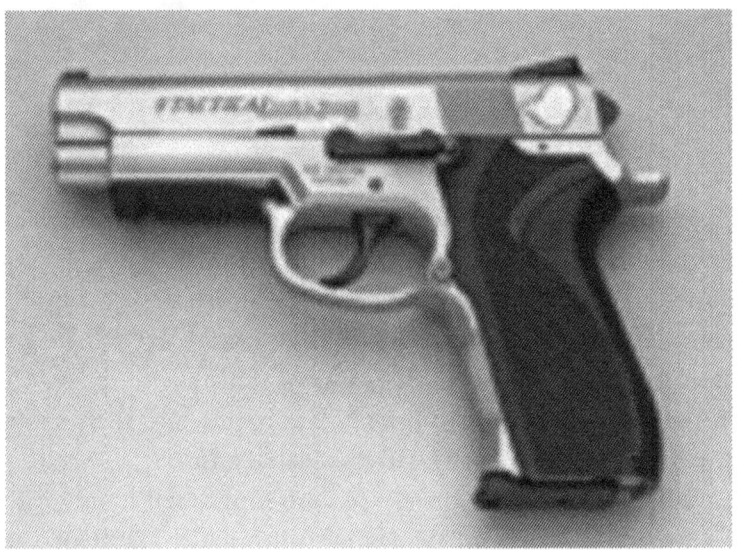

Although I do not own one of Smith & Wesson's large caliber semi-automatic pistols, I have fired them and found them to be very reliable. As I mentioned earlier, my competition .22 LR caliber was a Smith & Wesson model 41 and it was a superb pistol, and I found it very accurate. I wish I had been able to shoot to the pistol's capability.

Unfortunately, in a moment of insanity I sold it, my Colt "Gold Cup" National Match, my Colt Officer's Model, and my custom made gun box to a friend because I thought I was giving up competitive shooting.

Below is a photo of the S&W Model 41, one of the finest target pistols ever made.

I purchased mine in 1959. The only difference was that it had a muzzle compensator to reduce muzzle jump so that you could quickly acquire the target again. I don't know why Smith & Wesson dropped the feature. As I recall, it had a 7-3/8ths inch barrel, including the compensator. I loved the pistol! It is always a mistake to sell a good fire-arm. The money you get for it quickly evaporates, and then you are left without either the money or the irreplaceable gun.

Colt made the revolver below. They no longer sell handguns to the public, which is a dirty shame. They only made 1,200 of the Colt "Boa" in .357-magnum caliber, and only 600 in the 4" barrel length.

*Colt "Boa" .357 magnum caliber revolver with a 4-inch barrel and
Pachmyr grips*

The Boa was "Pythonized," that is, the interior parts were hand-fitted, polished, and great care was taken in the assembly, as was also true of the famous Python (Colt named several of their handguns after snakes). The main difference between the Boa and the Python was the mainspring. On the Python, it was a leaf spring while on the Boa it was a coil spring like that on their Trooper model. Later, they came up with another, very similar, firearm, which they called the King Cobra. It was of stainless steel, but was not as highly finished as the beautiful Boa.

I would be remiss if I didn't show here the famous Colt Python .357 magnum caliber revolver. It was produced in several barrel lengths—including six inch, four inch and two inch. I should have bought one when I had the chance. They are renowned for their accuracy and much prized. Also, no other manufacturer does a better, more beautiful job of bluing their top-of-the-line firearms than Colt's "Royal Blue."

This famous revolver remains a classic among double-action revolvers. World-renowned for speed and accuracy, the Python is hand-honed for smooth action. Unfortunately the Colt company has stopped selling handguns to the general public—except police and military—due to the prevalence of malicious lawsuits that are filed by gun-banners against firearms manufacturers when a firearm is used in a criminal act. Although they virtually always lose, the cost to the firearms manufacturers in defending themselves is great. The suggested retail price of a new Python, if you are a police officer, is well over $1,000 and so it is not inexpensive.

Python with 4-inch barrel

Python with 2-inch barrel

Another famous pistol is the Colt model 1911A1. It was introduced in 1911, and became the standard service pistol of the U.S. armed forces, along with the S&W model 10 Military and Police revolver. The .45 ACP caliber model 1911A1 is an improved version of the old 1911, and it saw service throughout the Second World War and Korean conflict. The 1911 served in the First World War. Due to constant wear and tear, many of the old pistols in use became "loose as a goose", but they were universally respected and were manufactured by several companies besides Colt. I have owned several versions of the Colt .45 auto, including an original model 1911 (recognizable by the straight backstrap, as opposed to the curved one shown below on the 1911A1. Springfield Armory manufactured my current one.

Colt .45 ACP caliber model 1911A1

A few years ago, Colt came out with a similar but much lower priced model referred to as the 1991. It looked more like the old original 1911.

Colt .45 ACP caliber model 1991

Then there is the top of the line, the Colt Gold Cup Trophy, which serious competitors in bullseye target shooting almost invariably treasure. The ammunition favored usually is the wad-cutter bullet, which is a notoriously bad round for loading smoothly into the firing chamber, due to its shape.

Typical wad-cutter bullet

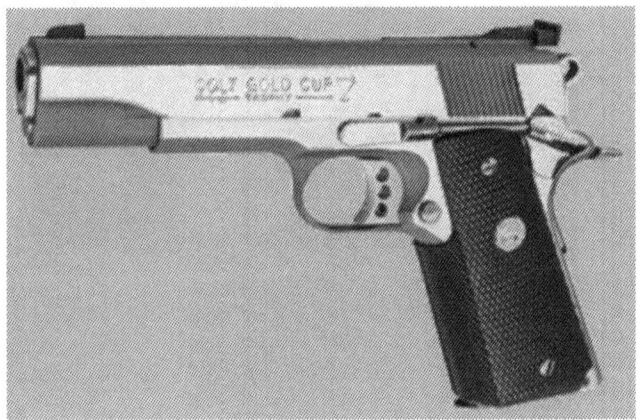

Colt Gold Cup Trophy—top of the line

The entrance to the chamber of the Gold Cup is polished and the ejection port is enlarged and polished, among other special features on this firearm. It enables it to handle wad-cutter bullets without problems. The reason many shooters prefer the wad-cutter is that it creates a perfectly round hole in the target, and is therefore much easier to score.

After eighty years or so of military service by the 1911, the United States adopted the 9 mm cartridge in order to conform to the typical ammunition of our NATO allies. Probably the old Colt could have been adapted to that cartridge, but the Pentagon, in its wisdom decided to replace the old war horse with another, more modern pistol—one of foreign manufacture—Go figure! Some of our most elite military units still favor the Colt model 1911A1 in .45 ACP caliber, however. Below is the pistol that replaced the Colt as the standard pistol of the U.S. military. The Beretta model 92F.

Beretta model 92F in 9 mm caliber

The Beretta is a fine Italian made pistol. Actually they are made under license in the United States, as well, as are many other products, such as Japanese automobiles, TVs, etc. Perhaps it is only sentiment, but I personally prefer the old Colt and its heftier caliber. It has been cloned by just about everyone. It is one of the three most instantly recognized guns in the world, and I own all three of them. The other two are the famous Luger and the Colt Single Action Army revolver. The Luger was first produced just before the beginning of the twentieth century, and the Colt SAA was introduced in 1873, so they are both centenarians. The Luger is commonly referred to as the "German Luger," but the name "Luger" has been owned by an American company, Stoeger Arms, since the 1920s. It's designer was a German, Georg Luger, who worked for the Deutsche Waffen und Munitionsfabriken (DWM) company. The legendary Hugo Borchardt designed the pistol that was the predecessor to the Luger. Many of the design features are nearly identical to those found on later Luger pistols. The 7.65 mm cartridge for which the Borchardt was designed hindered its military acceptance. It went out of production in 1899. Luger's redesign incorporated a 9 mm cartridge and the rest is history, as they say.

The "Naval Luger", referred to by the Germans as the Pistolen Model 04, with a 6-inch barrel

The German army adopted the Luger, with a 4-inch barrel, in 1908 four years after the navy had accepted the model P04. Both pistols were chambered for the 9mm cartridge. However, the Swiss army was the first to adopt the pistol, in 1900, ordering 3,000 for their military, and the United States government ordered 1,000 Lugers in 1901. About that same time DWM produced another 2,000 for the civilian market. All of these were produced in 7.65 mm (.30 caliber), like the Borchardt.

DWM Pistolen model 08 in 9mm

My own Luger was made in Houston, Texas, of stainless steel. It has the 6-inch barrel and was manufactured under contract to Stoeger. It is called the "American Eagle," and has the name "Luger" engraved on it in a wreath.

The "American Eagle" Naval Luger, 6-inch barrel, 9mm,
Stainless Steel, made in Houston, Texas, U.S.A.

The other of the triumvirate of famous pistols that more people on earth recognize on sight is the Colt model of 1873, known as the "Single Action Army" model, which is still being manufactured today as the "3ʳᵈ generation". It is still essentially the same revolver as the original, but no doubt the steel is vastly improved, as well as the fitting. Everyone who has ever watched an American Western movie has seen this gun, and that necessarily includes just about everyone on earth, I think. The majority of the most famous "cowboy" stars, Roy Rogers, Gene Autry, and of course John Wayne used them, and most of them, it seemed, tried to help the bullet on its way by "throwing" the old revolver down as they fired. Hollywood!

Third generation Colt SAA .45 Colt caliber

The unusual thing about the revolver in the picture above is that I got it in trade for a Government Model 1991 semi-automatic pistol. The pistol I traded for it cost me $550 new from a dealer at a gun show, and it was finished in Royal Blue, with Colt's trademark rampant colt inlaid in gold on the slide, and the words "Classic .45" on the slide in script lettering, also in gold. I had replaced the walnut grips it came with, with faux ivory handles. I was in my son's computer shop on the coast one day when a friend of his came in, saw the pistol, and wanted it. I told him the name of the dealer in Portland from whom I'd purchased it, and the price, but he wanted *that* gun, right now!

I told him, of course, that I didn't want to sell it, and he left. Shortly thereafter he returned with this beautiful SAA, unfired, new in the box, and a couple hundred bucks worth of leather (holster and belt.)

I couldn't refuse! We traded on the spot. The SAA's manufacturer's suggested retail at that time was, I think over $1,200. Now the gun sells new for close to $2,000. As I said, sometimes firearms are a good investment.

The Colt SAA has been cloned a lot, both by the Italians and other foreign manufacturers as well as many American companies. One of the good ones—actually a stronger gun than the Colt—is the Ruger "Vaquero." It has some extra safety features, such as a hammer block so that you can carry six rounds in the chamber, whereas in the Colt SAA it is recommended that you leave an empty chamber under the hammer to avoid an accidental discharge. If a cartridge is carried in that chamber, the firing pin rides directly on the primer in the Colt, but the Ruger has a floating firing pin and a hammer block so that it is actually necessary to pull the trigger for the gun to fire. Of course the Colt can be carried on half cock, but that is not a recommended safe carry.

And the Ruger's cost is considerably less than the Colt, largely because of the Colt's history and reputation, and the respective manufacturing methods the two companies use. Ruger uses the "lost wax" process, and molds their parts in molten steel, whereas Colt uses the traditional method of machining their parts. Below is a Ruger Vaquero (vaquero is the Spanish word from which was derived the American word "Buckaroo.")

Ruger "Vaquero" in .45 Colt caliber

In the Ruger Vaquero there is no firing pin protruding from the hammer; it is "floating" in the frame. On the Colt, the firing pin is attached to the hammer, and when the hammer is down it rides directly on the cartridge. If the hammer is bumped, or the revolver is dropped with a cartridge in the chamber under the hammer, it can fire.

That accounts for the three most universally recognized handguns on earth.

They are all pretty good-sized firearms; not as big as the powerful .44 magnum, which Clint Eastwood, as Detective Harry Callahan, characterized as the most powerful handgun on earth (which it is no longer), but the big .44 would be rather uncomfortable to carry concealed on your person, not only because of its size, but also its weight. Somewhat like concealing a cannon!

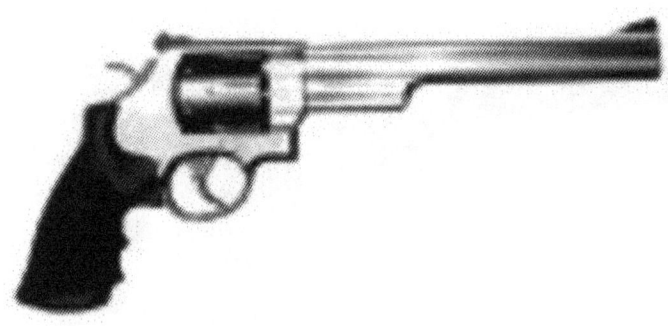

The S&W Model 29 .44 magnum revolver

A 2-1/2 pound firearm can be a lot of weight to carry around all day, whether it is on your hip, in your armpit, or anywhere else, let alone a 3-1/2 pounder!. Most of us want something lighter, like this little Colt "Pony" in .380 ACP caliber. It is flat, weighs only 13 ounces, and you can carry it without even being aware of it. Although it puts out less energy than a .38 Special, it has the same diameter bullet and at close range it does just fine to discourage an attacker.

Colt "Pony" .380 ACP caliber

This little pistol came, out of the box, with one of the hardest trigger pulls I've ever experienced. It was, as I recall, about twenty pounds. A weapon should have at least a 4-pound trigger, and they often run to a dozen or so pounds. I installed a new trigger spring, by Woolf, and had a local gunsmith give it a trigger job. Then, I rounded off all the hard edges so that I could carry it in my pocket without wearing out the fabric. The gun is primarily made of aluminum, which accounts for its light weight, although all of its important working parts are, of course, of steel. It is the gun I most often carry, and I usually use an inside-the-pants holster (pictured elsewhere), which I bought from Dillon Precision, in Arizona. They manufacture some of the finest hand-loading equipment on earth, and I am a fan of their company. I also sometimes carry in a specially made undershirt, which sports two holsters (one under each arm) when I am running around in hot weather with no jacket or sweater, and my shirt tucked in. Both methods make the firearm invisible to the public. These days people freak out if they think you are carrying, and brandishing (showing) a weapon is enough to cause to lose your permit to carry concealed in Oregon.

A nice little revolver, which I carried until I bought the Pony, is the diminutive Charter Arms "Bulldog" .357 magnum double-action revolver, which weighs in at about a pound. I also used an inside-the-pants holster for it, which I made. It is only a five-shooter, and so is almost as flat as an automatic. I load it with .38 Special cartridges, usually, since I worry about things like over-penetration. It is very comfortable to wear.

This was an infamous pistol in .44 Special caliber. The serial killer who was known as "Son of Sam" used it in his crime spree.

Charter Arms "Bulldog", .357-magnum caliber

The Bulldog doesn't have the smoothest trigger around, and is not as well honed on the interior as some of the top brands, but it has a solid frame (no side plates) and is well made. They are no longer available in this model. You'll have to find a used one. The original Charter Company is out of business, like many of the smaller manufacturers of good firearms. Probably they just didn't have a big enough treasury to withstand all of the legal attacks and the impact on their market of those whose intent it is to disarm America.

Other small firearms, which are easy to carry without drawing attention to yourself are the little derringers. As most people know, it was a Deringer (notice the different spelling), which John Wilkes Booth used to assassinate Abraham Lincoln. The designer of this small pistol actually spelled his name with a single 'r'. The pistols that bear the name these days are a different breed than the unwieldy weapon that killed Lincoln.

Derringers

I have two of them; the top one is an American Derringer in .38 Special caliber, and underneath it is a tiny Davis Firearms .32 ACP caliber gun. Each of them holds only two shots. They are minimal self-defense firearms, and I would not recommend relying upon them as your only means of protection. They are useful, though, as backups for carry in a pocket or an ankle holster. There are lots of other fine guns we could mention, but you can shop for them in the magazines and in your local gun store.

7

The Politics of Gun Control

Regardless of the Second Amendment, which all politicians on the federal level are required to take an oath to protect and defend since it is an integral part of the Constitution, there has been for the last few decades a concerted effort to disarm the American people, and to restrict their freedoms. Of course, as socialism progresses and the federal government gets farther and farther away from its Constitutional mandates and ever larger and more powerful, it inserts itself into every aspect of our lives. The people become ever more dependent, as new socialist programs are enacted to "benefit" them. First, it was Social Security, designed to prevent those who lacked the foresight to prepare adequately for their own retirement years from becoming destitute. The argument was, and always is, that the people, individually, are not thoughtful enough to take care of themselves, so "Big Brother" must do it for them.

Such a government treats its citizens as children—rather helpless children, really—who must be looked after and protected from themselves.

New programs arise almost daily, it seems. There was Medicare and Medicaid and all of the "Great Society" programs inaugurated by Lyndon Johnson's administration—and they all cost money; huge amounts of money. The cost, in the multi-trillions, closely paralleled the national debt. It is, of course the prodigal, wasteful, childlike, irresponsible people who must pay the freight. The very people that the government distrusts to take care of their own affairs.

When the income tax was inaugurated a member of the Congress is said to have protested, "*Now* it is one percent, but what is there to prevent it from going to two percent, or even three percent?" To which the reply was, "Don't be silly! The people would revolt!"

Now, taxes from all levels of government are taking half of the average citizen's paycheck, and still there is no revolt. Why not? Because back during Franklin Roosevelt's administration someone dreamed up the payroll deduction, and since then you pay your taxes without ever seeing the money. It didn't take politicians long to realize that when they take money from us that we have never seen, we don't miss it, and then the tax increases started going through the roof, and on their heels came a hugely powerful federal government—originally designed by the framers of the Constitution to be merely the agent for the sovereign states—and we began to see career politicians, whose primary agenda was to stay in office, and only secondarily to serve their constituency. "Tell them what they want to hear" became their motto.

Now, things have progressed so far that it is extremely unlikely that we shall ever again see constitutional government. The Constitution that our representatives in the Congress so blithely swear to uphold is seen by many of them as an archaic document that has no bearing on modern life. It is a thing to joke about.

But, the Constitution is no laughing matter, and in the Preamble, it states, *"We, the people of the United States, in order to form a more perfect Union, establish justice, insure domestic tranquility, provide for the common defense, promote the general welfare, and secure the blessings of liberty to ourselves and our posterity do ordain and establish this Constitution for the United States of America."*

It establishes in the first three words who the authors of the document are—and where the power rests. Next, it gives the goals of the document. It is the Constitution that creates the federal government, and the Constitution that designs that government and tells it what it may and may not do. But, the people in those days refused to ratify it until a Bill of Rights was added—a document within a document—that protected the people from the eventuality of an overweening government, like the one from which they had just won their freedom at a great cost in blood.

They certainly were not then cast as irresponsible or profligate. They wanted the government off their backs. They didn't want government to provide them with health care, or food, or clothing, or a roof over their heads. They didn't expect to be handed money in their old age. They wanted freedom—liberty!

In the Bill of Rights many things are addressed.

The First Amendment told Congress that it would not be allowed to make any law establishing a state religion or prohibiting the free exercise of religion; that it could not restrict speech, or a free press; that it could not prevent the people from assembling, nor could it prohibit them from petitioning the government for a redress of grievances.

The Second Amendment had only one subject, which rather signifies its priority to the framers: The right of the people to keep [own] and bear [carry] arms shall not be infringed *because* a militia is necessary to the security of a *free* state. A militia, at that time, was composed of all the people. And the people at that time despised having a standing army in their midst, having just gotten rid of one—the British.

The Constitution was not a legalistic document, requiring a lawyer to understand it. It was a contract between the people who designed it, and the government they were creating. It was written in plain English, for all to understand. They wanted their contract written down, on paper, so that there would never be any misunderstanding.

The Third Amendment simply said the people would not stand for soldiers to be quartered among them without their consent, in their houses, except in wartime, and even then only according to law.

These people really didn't want to be saddled with a standing army! They'd seen too much of it with the British living among them, lording it over them!

The Fourth Amendment forbade government to knock down their doors and invade their homes, yelling, "Federal agents! Federal agents! On the floor, M—rs!" Unreasonable searches and seizure of your property were out! They have to have a warrant, and there has to be probable cause before the magistrate can issue it. And, they have to describe the thing they are looking for in the warrant.

The Fifth Amendment is a big one, mainly about justice: The government has to have a Grand Jury indictment before it can try someone for a crime that could result in the death penalty, except in military cases; it can't try someone twice for the same offense; a person can't be made to testify against themselves; when you are tried, you have the right to confront the witnesses against you; you can't be deprived of life, liberty or property without a trial; they can't take your property for public use simply by condemning it and grabbing it—they have to pay you a fair price for it.

Can you think of any cases recently where any of these rights have been violated by our federal government?

Like the Fifth Amendment, **The Sixth Amendment** is about the pursuit of justice; it requires that in all criminal prosecutions, the accused has a right to a speedy trial—none of this languishing in jail for months or even years until they get around to trying you! The jury that tries you has to be impartial and composed of people just like you (your peers) and the trial has to be in the same venue in which the alleged crime took place; in addition, the accused has a right to full information as to the accusation and the facts against him or her, and to a counsel to assist with his defense.

The Seventh Amendment is also about the procedures to secure justice. In suits of common law (civil suits) where the amount in question is over $20 the right of trial by jury shall be preserved, and once the jury decides on the facts, those facts cannot be re-examined by any court in the United States.

The Eighth Amendment simply states that there shall not be any excessive bail, excessive fines, nor cruel and unusual punishment inflicted. Those are not defined, and there have been unending arguments in those areas. Many maintain that the death penalty is cruel and unusual, but it was common at the time the Constitution was written and it's hard to believe that the framers included it in that category.

The Ninth and Tenth Amendments are significant and important, but in recent times have increasingly been smiled at by those who represent us in the Congress. The Ninth simply says that just because the Constitution delineates certain rights, that doesn't mean that those are *all* the rights the people have. The Tenth is succinct, clear, and to the point. It says, in plain English that cannot be misunderstood:

> *"The powers not delegated to the United States, nor prohibited by it to the States, are reserved to the States respectively, or to the people."*

If the Constitution doesn't tell the federal government it can do it, or if it doesn't prohibit the States from doing it, then that right belongs to the State, or to the people. Pretty clear, wouldn't you say?

The way the federal government gets around that one is by buying the state's compliance. They hand out money—that you and I paid in taxes—to get our state to go along with their highway scheme, or their school program, or whatever other nefarious scheme they have.

The Bill of Rights guarantees the citizenry the rights delineated above, but what good are rights if your elected servants pay no attention to them. What good are rights if your employees, the anonymous government bureaucrats, step all over them with rules and procedures which deny them. For example, let us say that you are a citizen of Greek descent and the federal government decides to put you in a concentration camp along with all other citizens of Greek descent without a trial?

That couldn't happen, you say? How about the time when the federal government, by edict, imprisoned all American citizens of Japanese descent in 1942, for the duration of the war, and confiscated their property, without trial.

Things like that can, and do happen.

The Second Amendment has been called the palladium of the Bill of Rights—that which affords protection or security; a safeguard—it gives the people teeth to defend their rights against overweening politicians and external enemies.

I doubt that most of those who would disarm the people of the United States, and deny them their birthright, are un-American in their hearts. I think that most of them are well-meaning patriotic citizens who simply have not thought through what it is they are trying to do. Well-meaning, but misinformed and misled. It is quite obvious that most of them are political liberals who register as Democrats—at least it is their representatives in Congress who introduce most of the anti-gun legislation: Charles Schumer of New York, Dianne Feinstein of California, Hillary Clinton of New York, Teddy Kennedy of Massachusetts and all of their sycophants and followers—and they continue to elect them! There are also some liberal Republicans who are too willing to follow the gun-control fanatics.

If we lose the battle, and we are required by law to hand in our firearms, we will go the same way as have England, Australia and Canada: crime rates will increase because only law-abiding people will obey the law and turn in their firearms. It follows that the only ones left with firearms will be the military, the police—and the outlaws. Then, it will be too late.

There is a powerful drive in the United Nations to introduce a worldwide ban on the private ownership of firearms. The Clinton Administration was all for it. Bill Clinton was the most anti-gun president in the history of this nation, besides being the most amoral man to ever sit in the Oval Office.

There are those who would have us give up our national sovereignty and give in to the United Nations, and adopt their proscriptions, flouting our Bill of Rights and giving up our form of government completely, a system which has been good enough, in spite of any perceived flaws, to allow us to become the strongest nation on earth, and the haven that most other peoples seek when the going gets too rough in their own land.

The cruelest blow of all is the hatred for the United States that persists in some of the very countries that we saved from Nazi tyranny in the Second World War, and afterward spent billions on in reconstruction. It just goes to show that peoples to whom you give an unearned handout, no matter whether it is the welfare recipient at home, or the foreign people who were starving, that learn to resent their saviors. A sure way to gain an enemy is to demonstrate your superiority by giving them a handout.

Why do we concentrate on handguns? Because they are portable and concealable. The people can arm themselves unobtrusively, and tyrants fear an armed people, which is why the first action of someone like Hitler is always to register the people's guns, and the second deed is to confiscate them.

In the Warsaw Ghetto, when the German SS had control and were starving the Jewish inhabitants and sending them to concentration camps for annihilation, a resistance sprang up among the Jews. They were initially armed with only ten handguns, but they held off the entire German army for three months. They procured more firearms by killing Germans. Their example shows what a ragtag group of rebels can do with a few handguns, in the face of tyranny.

The current spate of gun-control laws in the United States started shortly after the Nuremberg War Criminal Trials following the Second World War. There is hard evidence to indicate that the German Weapons Law of March 18, 1938, is the source of the U.S. Gun Control Act of 1968 (GCA '68). Adolph Hitler signed the Nazi Weapons Law and his Secret Police enforced it. The Jews for the Preservation of Firearms Ownership (JPFO) did a side-by-section comparison of the GCA '68 with the Nazi Weapons Law. They say they know who implanted the German (Nazi) weapons law into American law.

The likely culprit is a former U.S. Senator, now deceased. Senator Thomas Dodd, a Democrat from Connecticut had served as senior member of the U.S. team that helped to prosecute Nazi war criminals at Nuremberg, and brought back with him a copy of the Nazi gun law. As Chairman of the Senate Subcommittee of the Judiciary Committee to Investigate Juvenile Delinquency, he was the prime mover to get the Gun Control Act of 1968 (GCA 68) signed into law. Why would any U.S. Senator want to implant Nazi law into the United States? It is almost unbelievable. And yet, a close comparison between the two documents leaves no room for doubt. That is exactly what happened. GCA 68 is the law which introduced the idea that firearms must have a "legitimate sporting use," and forbade the interstate transportation of legal firearms, which effectively ended mail order sales to law abiding citizens unless they held a dealers license.

It also opened the door for Washington bureaucrats to ban the importation of whole classes of firearms, which they have enthusiastically done ever since.

The Nazi Weapons Law of 1938 replaced the German Law on Firearms dated April 13, 1928. A freely elected German government that wanted to stop violent street fights between Nazi brown shirts and Communist thugs created the 1928 law. It required that all firearm owners and their firearms had to be registered. Familiar words?

The Nazis inherited lists of firearms owners and when they took over the government in 1933, they used the registration lists to seize privately held firearms since they knew exactly where to find them.

They next restricted firearms ownership to only party members, thus barring all Jews from owning the means to protect themselves from tyranny; even clubs or knives. The sharp parallels between GCA 68 and the Nazi Weapons Law indicate that the framers of the American law, lacking any legal basis in this country to infringe on our civil rights, used the Nazi law as a guide to achieve their ends. They obviously admired Hitler's law! They of course had to flout the Constitution in so doing, but *C'est la Vie!*

A letter from a librarian at the Library of Congress exists that states that the late Senator Thomas J. Dodd personally owned a copy of the original German text of the Nazi Weapons Law, and that he, the librarian, translated it into English for him shortly before GCA 68 was introduced.

Why did Dodd own the original German text of any Nazi law? Why did he make known that he owned it?

One thing becomes obvious from all of this; there are people in the United States, and many of them are in our Congress, elected by us, who are bent upon eliminating our rights as spelled out in our Constitution. People who are *sworn to uphold and defend* the Constitution! And the American people continue to elect some of them, time after time! I find that most disturbing of all, for it indicates that, at least in some sections of the country the people themselves are not well informed about our system of government and the Bill of Rights, or they would not repeatedly elect those who would destroy it.

It is not simply the Second Amendment that is under attack! There are repeated encroachments on the other nine amendments, as well. The reason that the Second Amendment is so important is that it is our Last Resort against tyranny!

"Those who would give up essential Liberty, to purchase a little temporary safety, deserve neither Liberty nor safety."

—Benjamin Franklin

8

The Media and Gun Control

The elite media—that is, those organizations who operate on a national level and who supply national news to America's daily newspapers and local television stations—have an earned reputation for being politically liberal, and for slanting the news they supply so that it represents their views. They include the *New York Times*, the *Washington Post, The Los Angeles Times, USA Today*, the Associated Press, and virtually all of the major television networks except, perhaps the Fox network.

NBC, ABC, CBS and of course the Clinton News Network (CNN) all have a left-wing slant. Public Radio and Television is also a left-wing sycophant with a notorious anti-gun slant.

Fortunately, for those on the other side of the political spectrum there are alternatives: the various neutral news websites on the World Wide Web, many local radio and television stations, and a few courageous newspapers and magazines, like the *Washington Times, National Review,* and a few others with a national readership. But generally, the public is fed a continuous diet of liberal claptrap, and so the occasional conservative voice is welcome, indeed. Voices like Rush Limbaugh, who has the largest daily audience of anyone, on radio or TV, and Larry Elder, and Sean Hannity, and Barry Farber—and there are several others. They are a breath of fresh air in an otherwise tainted atmosphere.

One wonders why the media elite is so universally liberal—sometimes so left wing they approach communist philosophy—and I think it is probably a combination of factors.

They no doubt think it is because they are more intelligent than the "redneck rabble" in flyover country that call themselves conservative.

Probably it goes back to the journalism schools, where the faculty is predominantly liberal, and in fact were a primary target for communist infiltrators a few decades ago where their young students had little life experience to draw on and thus their BS meters were not yet functioning. I knew one such professor well, and his political orientation was a little left of Lenin's. He hated capitalism.

Then another factor comes in: the motive for choosing journalism for their life's work in the first place. Most journalists I have met, and there have been several, were idealists. Their motive was not simply to report the news, but to change what they perceived as the flaws of society, which usually means, "helping the underdog." They would like to see free medical care for everyone, hang the cost! No one should go hungry in this great, rich land! They usually hold the opinion that the "giant corporations" are bad, and the rich should not have all that money! Surely not while the poor are hurting, anyway.

It reminds me of the story of the ant and the grasshopper, which someone sent me by e-mail:

The Classic Version

The ant works hard in the withering heat all summer long, building his house and laying up supplies for the winter. The grasshopper, on the other hand, thinks he's a fool, and laughs and dances and plays the summer away.

Come winter, the ant is warm and well fed. The grasshopper has no food or shelter, so he dies out in the cold.

The Modern Version

The ant works hard in the withering heat all summer long, building his house and laying up supplies for the winter. The grasshopper, on the other hand, thinks he's a fool, and laughs and dances and plays the summer away.

Come winter, the shivering grasshopper calls a press conference and demands to know why the ant should be allowed to be warm and well fed while others less fortunate are cold and starving.

CBS, NBC and ABC show up to provide pictures of the shivering grasshopper next to a video of the ant in his comfortable home with a table filled with food.

America is stunned by the sharp contrast. How can this be, that in a country of such wealth, this poor grasshopper is allowed to suffer so?

Kermit the Frog appears on Oprah with the grasshopper and everybody cries when they sing, "It's Not Easy Being Green".

Jesse Jackson stages a demonstration in front of the ant's house, where the news stations film the group singing, "We shall overcome".

Al Gore exclaims in an interview with Peter Jennings that the ant has gotten rich off the back of the grasshopper and calls for an immediate tax hike on the ant to make him pay his "fair share".

Finally, the EEOC drafts the "Economic Equity and Anti-Grasshopper Act" retroactive to the beginning of the summer.

The ant is fined for failing to hire a proportionate number of green bugs and, having nothing left to pay his retroactive taxes, his home is confiscated by the government.

Hillary gets her old law firm to represent the grasshopper in a defamation suit against the ant, and the case is tried before a panel of federal judges that Bill appointed from a list of single-parent welfare recipients. The ant loses the case.

The story ends as we see the grasshopper finishing up the last bits of the ant's food while the government house he is in, which just happens to be the ant's old house, crumbles around him because he doesn't maintain it. The ant has disappeared in the snow.

The grasshopper is found dead in a drug related incident and the house, now abandoned, is taken over by a gang of spiders who terrorize the once peaceful neighborhood.

The End

Such people just naturally gravitate to socialism. They want not equality of opportunity, but equality of *result*. To them, if you have more than me, it is your duty to share it with me.

It was people like that who dreamed up the graduated income tax. It was slogans about such disparity between the rich and the poor, that created American communists in the 'twenties.

The thing they leave out, when they attack the "giant corporations," is the fact that you and I own them. When we buy into a mutual fund, we become capitalists!

In any event, there seems to be a combination of factors at work that produces like-mindedness among journalists so that all of the talking heads on television news, and virtually all of the editorials in the newspapers, with rare exceptions, and many of the news commentators share similar views. And the common view is blatantly liberal, and anti-gun, and it shows.

A great conspiracy? No way! That would require secrecy, and there is too much competition for the ratings on TV and in the newspaper business. I don't think a conspiracy is even possible, except perhaps the initial one by the Comintern when they first began their infiltration of our institutions, which was no secret.

During the cold war, the cold-eyed, card carrying communists referred to such fellow travelers as, "useful idiots". In any case, we are stuck with the situation at least for the foreseeable future, and we must learn to live with it. Most of us have done so already, and ignore the network news and the wire service and the syndicated news from the elite media, except on non-political matters.

After one lives a few decades, you develop a BS detector, and it works overtime when you are watching or reading the news.

One of the phrases that strikes the suspicion chord is the statement, "Many experts say..." or, "According to the experts..." Others are "sources within the (Pentagon) (White House)..." One suspects that when a reporter is making something up on the spot, or expressing his or her personal opinion, that is the method of choice.

Another thing is statistics. Statistics can be, and often are, twisted to suit the speaker's own ends. It is true that there are lies, damned lies, and statistics. An editor friend told me once, "ninety percent of all statistics printed in this paper were made up on the spot, including this one."

How about those "experts" the media depend upon for technical advice. Remember the Alar scare? It nearly put the Wenatchee Valley of Washington state, world famous for its apples, out of business.

The Natural Resources Defense Council, Ralph Nader and Meryl Streep decided, based upon their vast expertise, that the chemical Alar, a brand name for the chemical daminozide, made by the Uniroyal Chemical Company for use as a pesticide on apples, pears and peaches, was a dangerous carcinogen. The news services leapt on it! Schools stopped serving apples, grocers posted signs that their apples were "Alar free," and Washington apple growers were going broke by the hundreds.

But Gilbert Ross, medical director for the American Council on Science and Health in Washington, contends the original reporting on Alar was distorted. "You don't need protection from non-threats such as this," said Ross, whose public health consumer-advocacy group accepts contributions from both corporations and not-for-profit foundations. "We need protection from environmentalists' hysterics."

Consumer activist Ralph Nader and actress Meryl Streep urged a ban on Alar. The furor cost apple growers across the country more than $100 million in reduced sales from their $1 billion crop. An undetermined number of growers went out of business or switched to other varieties or crops. At the time, only about 15 percent of U.S. apple growers were believed to be using Alar, but all were tarred by the panic's broad brush. "The government wasn't able to respond about the safety of apple products," recalls Wally Ewart, vice president for scientific affairs for the Northwest Horticultural Council in Yakima. "It did not come out quickly and say we're ensuring a safe food supply."

The point of all this is that the environmentalists were wrong, the Natural Resources Defense Council was shown to be a reactionary environmentalist group, more political than scientific and yet the news agencies grabbed the "news" they dished out eagerly and disseminated it all over the country for them.

And here's the denouement: the Natural Resources Defense Council still, to this day, is treated as a respected source of "expert" advice by the elite media. You see quotes from them every day in the newspaper. Did they lose credibility with their left wing chums in the press? No way!

The elite media are strong defenders of gun control. They get most of their figures and views from Sarah Brady's Center to Prevent Handgun Violence, an offshoot of Handgun Control, Inc. Their misinformation and skewed figures are notorious. We'll look at some of them later, and the answers to them, in another chapter.

You would think that the news media would look to the National Rifle Association for accurate figures and advice on firearms. The NRA has been around since 1871, and has received grateful thanks from at least two presidents, following the First and Second World Wars for their efforts. Also, they have claimed two Congressional Medal of Honor holders (the nation's highest award) as their president, the latest being Joe Foss, a Marine Corps fighter pilot in the Second World War, who shot down twenty-six Japanese aircraft while he was based at Henderson Field in Guadalcanal in 1942. When he returned to the Unites States, he was elected as Governor of South Dakota, and subsequently became President of the NRA.

As an interesting aside, a few months ago, following the September 11, 2001, terrorist attacks, airline security was "beefed up," as they say.

Joe Foss was traveling by air to deliver a speech to the military cadets at West Point, and so had his Congressional Medal of Honor with him to show them. Airport security stopped him because of a metal plate in his body, had him remove his boots twice, and wanted to take his Congressional Medal of Honor away from him. They didn't recognize the medal! This is security? A war hero in his late seventies, past governor of one of the United States, is mistaken for a terrorist! How many of the actual terrorists fitted that description, on the Eleventh of September, 2001?

As Shakespeare observed, in *Julius Caesar,* "O judgment, thou art fled to brutish beasts and men have lost their reason!"

The NRA has a firearms museum including one of the greatest collections of historical firearms in existence, and their membership includes more genuine firearms experts than any other organization anywhere. They have a membership of nearly five million shooters, a small representation of the approximately 80 million gun owners in the United States, at last estimate, who own probably 200 million firearms of various descriptions.

If the great number of gun owners ever realize the danger that they face of losing their treasured firearms to confiscation by the anti-gun forces, if the enemies of the Bill of Rights in the Congress should reach a majority, they could easily control an election with their votes. Because of that, the gun-control faction treads lightly at election time, stating that they really only want to keep guns from the hands of the criminals, and save the children, and they really want to preserve the right to bear arms by honest, law-abiding citizens who like to go duck hunting.

The Second Amendment was not written to protect duck hunting or recreation. The men who wrote it knew that it was serious business.

The liberal faction in Congress will keep trying to disarm America, and the liberal press will continue to support them. The National Rifle Association, the Gun Owners of America, the RKBA, the JPFO and other such organizations will keep spreading the word to those who will listen, and the uninformed and those who, out of ignorance, fear firearms will continue to vote for those who would destroy the Bill of Rights and, with it, the Constitution of the United States and all that it represents that our people have fought and died for down through the centuries. In one generation, ennui, ignorance and the apathy of our citizens could undo what our enemies have failed to accomplish in over 200 years.

9

The Second Amendment And the Courts

I n the year 1671, about the time my first colonial ancestor, Thomas Pier, came to this country from England and settled in Lyme, Connecticut, King Charles II ordered that all indigent Englishmen be disarmed, and his governor in Virginia set about to accomplish that aim. It was an attempt to subjugate his subjects in the poor and middle classes as well as certain religious groups, the Irish, Scots, and the American Indians. A death penalty was inaugurated for supplying firearms to Indians.

Governor Sir William Berkeley complained how miserable his job was when six out of seven of his people were "poore, endebted, discontented and armed." A tough job, indeed.

Americans have, throughout our history, taken private arms as our birthright, until this present generation. The battle of Lexington was a good example of what early Americans thought of their guns.

At daybreak on April 19th, the church bells rang alarm as Major Pitcairn's detachment marched into town. His plans to disarm the populace had been leaked, and the people were ready for him. Armed with rifles, they faced his infantry across the square. After an uneasy pause, the Major lost patience and charged.

Eight Americans were killed and ten wounded that day in 1775 at Lexington by their own army, which heavily outnumbered them, but the militia forced the British army to withdraw.

Of the 220 million people killed in the twentieth century, their own governments, according to a recent article in *National Review* magazine, killed 115 million. Other sources place governmental murders as low as 65 million. In Germany, the Soviet Union, China, Cambodia, Ethiopia, Somalia, Haiti, Nicaragua, El Salvador, Uganda, Rwanda, Iran, Iraq, Yugoslavia, over and over the same story: the defenseless, the unarmed, the helpless are slaughtered by their own despotic rulers.

Tyrannical government is a common phenomenon. James Madison, author of the Bill of Rights, assured Americans that they need never fear their new government because of "the advantage of being armed, which you possess over the people of almost every other nation." (Today perversely used as an argument to disarm us.)

Aristotle recognized that tyrants "mistrust the people; hence they deprive them of arms." A notable exception is little Switzerland, where virtually all able-bodied males undergo military training and are issued submachine-guns, which they keep in their homes. Not surprisingly, they enjoy one of the lowest crime rates on earth.

Anti-gunners like the Center to Prevent Handgun Violence and their liberal politician buddies in Congress and the media elite also claim that acquaintances are shot more often than strangers. No doubt true: dope-dealers and rival gang members know each other. Another favorite is the old refrain about "children" shooting each other, referring to young inner-city thugs (under twenty-one) engaging in gang warfare. The rare child tragedy from careless gun storage is seized upon by the liberal press and results in headlines. They claim that abuse of the Second Amendment right causes violence, but neglect to mention the primary cause: abuse of the First Amendment. We are bathed in depraved sex and violence in the movies, television "entertainment," magazines and lurid novels. The First Amendment protects pornography, they say, but not political speech. Check out the Campaign Finance Reform Act.

Today, sophist cynics guffaw and titter at an Oregon legislator who proposed a law requiring households to have firearms, which she introduced while acknowledging self-consciously that it was her "one wild thing." Well, let them sneer and smirk. The mostly urbanite liberals who feed the anti-gun movement are also the source of crusaders for fewer and shorter prison terms, and blame crime on the weapon, the parents, the culture—anything except the criminal.

In fact, when Morton Grove, Illinois, passed a law banning hand-guns, the town of Kennesaw, Georgia, passed an ordinance similar to that proposed by Liz VanLeeuwen. Which town do you think had a marked reduction in crime, and which saw an increase? Right! Morton Grove's crime went through the roof, and Kennesaw's dropped to vir-tually nothing.

Gun-grabbers theorize that their proposed gun-control laws, of which there are 20,000 in the United States, would reduce violence, but nowhere in history is there a single instance in fact to back up that claim, though there are plenty of examples to justify the *opposite*. The reason is obvious: people who use firearms in crime do not respect law,

Do you want to slow down violence, control the drug-dealing gangs, and stop the grinning rioters from burning our cities? Let's go back to our heritage, the self-armed, mufti-clad militia, with elected neighborhood officers, and regular drills and trained in advance, as a militia or a trained and drilled ("well ordered?") neighborhood watch.

Not such a wild idea, Liz!

Although we hire police, we are ourselves ultimately responsible for domestic tranquility. Outraged cries of "vigilantes!" directed at those who armed themselves against the mobs during the Los Angeles riots are nonsense: The original vigilantes lynched suspects—the armed citizens in Los Angeles protected themselves in the absence of police. They would have been more effective had they been organized and trained in advance, as a militia or a trained and drilled ("well ordered?") neighborhood watch. The first cases of gun control in recent history probably were the more-or-less understandable attempts by lawmen like Wyatt Earp to prevent the cowboys fresh from a cattle drive from carrying their pistols in town, because they tended to drink and go hog wild after months on the trail, like all young men tend to do away from home, with no one to hold them accountable. The saloon keepers and bawdy houses welcomed their trade, as long as they stayed on their side of the tracks! The West, however, was never as deadly as the more populous cities in the East with their immigrant ghettos, gangs of thugs, racial tensions and all the other residual effects of overcrowding.

The United States v. Miller

The first and best-known Second Amendment case to come to the attention of the U.S. Supreme Court in the last century was probably *U.S. v. Miller* (1939), a case often cited by the anti-gunners as a victory for their cause. Actually, it was not. In fact, it is probably the nearest the Supreme Court has come to a direct construction of the Second Amendment as it was written.

In this particular case, two bootleggers were arrested by the Alcohol and Tobacco Tax boys ("revenuers", now known as the Bureau of Alcohol, Tobacco and *Firearms*) who had set out to arrest them for making moonshine, but upon searching their operation, they found only sugar. Then, one of the revenuers noticed a shortened shotgun, which made it illegal according to a new federal law which had just been passed by Congress making possession of "sawed off" shotguns and automatic weapons, like the "Tommy" gun, illegal unless the owner first procured a $200 license and was approved by the Treasury Department. In other words, it was simply a tax matter.

The same law was used as an excuse a few years ago to attack the Branch Davidian's commune at Waco, Texas, resulting in the deaths of nearly 100 men, women and children. An informer told the Bureau of Alcohol, Tobacco and Firearms that the residents of the commune had obtained automatic firearms, but in the smoking rubble of the aftermath of the raid, none were found. It was all about taxes! They stormed the commune with guns blazing, and finally torched it because they thought someone had failed to pay the $200 license fee!

The 1934 law was passed in direct response to the private ownership of "Tommy guns" by hoodlums during prohibition, and the havoc they caused with them. It was patently unconstitutional because it infringed upon the right to keep and bear arms. The crooks' lawyer won in the Appellate Court, the two bootleggers were released, and the government appealed the decision to the Supreme Court, who agreed to hear the case.

Understandably, the bootleggers, who had been freed, never showed—nor did their lawyer—so there was no one to argue for the defense, and the government had a walk in the park. The Supreme Court, with no arguments to the contrary, ruled, "*In the absence of any evidence tending to show that possession or use of a 'shotgun having a barrel of less than eighteen inches in length' at this time has some reasonable relationship to the preservation or efficiency of a well regulated militia, we cannot say that the Second Amendment guarantees the right to keep and bear such an instrument. Certainly it is not within judicial notice that this weapon is any part of the ordinary military equipment or that its use could contribute to the common defense.*"

The Germans would have been surprised; during the First World War they so hated the old Winchester Model '97 pump action shotguns with short (20-inch) barrels, which American troops were using as "trench brooms," that they summarily executed any of our soldiers caught so armed. And, the Thompson submachine gun, of course, was certainly "ordinary military equipment," no doubt about that! And, although unaddressed, it was encompassed in the same law. And, we have been stuck with that law ever since, on the basis of a court case which the government won by default.

On the basis of that case, decided because of the Court's faulty information and lack of adequate research, we have been saddled with an unconstitutional law ever since.

And we've already discussed the Nazi Weapons law, which became our Gun Control Act of 1968 (GCA 68), thanks to the efforts of a U.S. Senator who admired the Nazis approach to disarming the people. It is clearly unconstitutional, but has not yet been addressed by the Court. Little by little, step-by-step, they make their advances, gradually reducing our freedoms while we stand by without protest. Had it been shown to the Court in *United States v. Miller*, that the shotgun was indeed "usual military equipment," the Court's wording clearly suggests that the weapon's possession by an individual would have been constitutional, and the law would have been knocked into a cocked hat, as it should have been.

Presser v. Illinois

The anti-gunners always claim that the Supreme Court has consistently ruled that the Second Amendment is not an individual right, but protects the right of the government to maintain a well-regulated militia, which, they say, has been replaced in recent years by the National Guard. Nothing could be farther from the truth! If that were so it would be the only amendment in the entire Bill of Rights that protected the rights of the government rather than the people *from* the government.

The nineteenth century case, *Presser v, Illinois* (1886), often cited by the anti-gunners as a demonstration of that view, is a good example of the misinformation they dish out to the public.

Presser was not about the individual right to arms, as they claim, but about a ban on parading a private gun-toting organization on the city streets. During the period in question the government—using the National Guard and occasionally the U.S. Army to bully the people, whereas the militia had always served to protect them—typically engaged in violent means to suppress labor unions, and so the labor unions fought back by forming self-defense organizations. They were not interested in overthrowing the government, simply in defending themselves *from* their government and exercising their right to bargain collectively with their employers for better wages and working conditions.

In response to the unions' self-defense organizations, Illinois legislated a ban on parading armed bodies of men on the city streets. They forbade "armed bodies of men to associate together as military organizations, or to drill or parade with arms in cities and towns unless authorized by law."

A group of German immigrants subsequently staged a parade in which they carried *unloaded* rifles, and were prosecuted as being in violation of that law, which the defendants claimed was obviously unconstitutional, being a clear violation of their First Amendment right to freely assemble, and their Second Amendment right to bear arms.

The Court, however, upheld the law, stating that it "does not infringe the right of the people to keep and bear arms" because, "The exercise of this power by the States is necessary to the public peace, safety and good order. To deny the power would be to deny the right of the States to disperse assemblages organized for sedition and treason, and the right to suppress armed mobs bent on riot and rapine."

Note that the people become a "mob" in the view of the Court when they try to protect themselves against an overweening government.

The Court also stated that they had previously ruled that the entire Bill of Rights, including the Second Amendment, "is a limitation only upon the power of Congress and the National Government, and not upon that of the States."

The implication of the ruling is clearly that the Bill of Rights only protected the people from federal laws, and not against state law. So, the gun-banners reason, the barrier to gun-control by the states is lifted, and the collective right to bear arms was knocked down by the Court.

The Supreme Court has, in fact, made some bad rulings, as epitomized by the infamous Dred Scott decision. This is not one of their most notable examples of judicial wisdom, either. It would seem that they were totally ignoring the Fourteenth Amendment, which was ratified in 1868, twenty years prior to *Presser*, and which specifically states that, "No State shall make or enforce any law which shall abridge the privileges or immunities of citizens of the United States," in effect making the states abide by the Bill of Rights, too. The Fourteenth Amendment was created as a direct result of some Southern states infringing on the constitutional rights of returning black soldiers to keep and bear the arms they were allowed to keep upon separation from the service.

However, the Constitution, in Article One, Section Eight, gives the U.S. Congress some power over the militia—they may call it up under certain conditions, and regulate its training to a certain degree—and in the *Presser* decision the Court observed that even if there were no Second Amendment the states were not empowered to disarm the people because that would deprive the Congress of the above powers, and thus of the services of the militia to maintain the peace. They further stated that the states may not "prohibit the people from keeping and bearing arms" and that the militia is not a select, uniformed organization, but it consists of "all citizens capable of bearing arms."

So, even in *Presser*, the Supreme Court, far from deciding in favor of gun-control, upheld the right of the people, individually, to keep and bear arms as elements of the militia, which is made up of all the people capable of bearing arms. And, there goes the whole case of the anti-gunners, right out the window. In other words, the Second Amendment means exactly what it says. Surprise, surprise!

Thanks to David Kopel for bringing the above case to my attention.

There are innumerable cases from individual states that can be, and have been cited as well as those of the Supreme Court.

Several years ago, I contacted the National Rifle Association, and asked them point blank why they did not find a classic, archetypical, clear case of a violation of the Second Amendment by government, and pursue it all the way to the Supreme Court of the United States, thereby stopping the argument in its tracks. I received a letter from someone (I've forgotten the name) in their legal department who gave me the answer. Essentially, he said that they could not be sure of a favorable outcome. At that time, it was a predominantly liberal court, and the NRA did not wish to provoke a bad decision and thus be instrumental in destroying the Second Amendment.

From that I must draw the conclusion that realistically, in the final analysis, we are at the mercy of the *political philosophies* of the nine judges of the Supreme Court, rather than the profound words of the framers of the Constitution as it was written. The judges decide for us what the Bill of Rights says, and means, although its words are in plain English for anyone to read. Something is rotten in Denmark when our freedoms hang from so tenuous a thread. Next month, the complexion of the Court might change, and they might decide that the Bill of Rights applies only to free, white, male landowners—who were originally the only ones who had the franchise in New England! In such an event, how could we respond? If they decide that it is constitutional to disarm us, regardless of the words of the Second Amendment, what is to prevent them from depriving us of our First Amendment rights, as well as the Second Amendment? What recourse would we have?

Think about it!

It doesn't take a lawyer, or a Court, to decipher the Constitution. It was not written in the legalese that lawyers so love. It was written in plain language—the language of the day—although it is a given that our language has evolved since that time, it is still plain and easy to understand.

The Second Amendment gives the people teeth! It is our final recourse against overweening politicians and tyrants. That is why it was included in the Bill of Rights.

The protection of our freedoms cannot be delegated to the courts or anyone else. They are our responsibility, and we must protect them. We must insist that our elected representatives and judges abide by them. All evil needs to triumph is for good men to do nothing.

10

Myths and Misstatements

G ary Kleck, PhD, and an eminent Florida criminologist, has spent several years studying the phenomena of the use of firearms for self-protection. He started out as a liberal who favored gun control but the results of his studies brought him around to the opposite viewpoint. Now, he is an advocate of an armed populace.

Dr. Kleck estimates that there are approximately two million cases each year of defensive gun use by Americans. His methodology was to actually question hundreds of people, privately, and to extrapolate, using that sample, to a nationwide figure. His methodology was statistically valid and is generally accepted by other statisticians, except, of course, those of the anti-gun persuasion. Subsequent to his study, the National Crime Victimization Survey made another study in which they estimated that only 108,000 such defensive uses of handguns occurred each year. When Dr. Kleck was questioned about the disparity of result, he responded that the NCVS was a non-anonymous government survey conducted by the Bureau of the Census. The interviewees were required to identify themselves to the interviewers and were told that the interviews were being conducted on behalf of the Department of Justice—the law enforcement branch of the government! In other words, they were told that they were speaking, in effect, to a law enforcement agency and that they were identified and could be contacted again at will. Since 88 percent of people who use firearms to defend themselves do so away from home, often in a location where it is illegal even to have a gun in one's possession—for example, in New York City—they would be confessing to a crime by admitting that they defended themselves with a firearm. The result? They simply didn't respond truthfully.

Dr. Kleck stands by his own assessment of the numbers of people who use firearms to protect themselves.

When Florida enacted legislation in 1987 allowing its citizens to carry concealed firearms providing that they had a clean record, no history of mental illness, and after passing a safety course, the anti-gun critics had a field day! They predicted gunfights over fender-benders, and generally increased rates of violence. They labeled Florida the "Gunshine" state, replacing its former appellation, the "Sunshine State." Of course, it never happened. The crime rates, instead of rising, dropped much faster than the national average. Only one permit holder, out of 350,000 issued, was convicted of a homicide through the ten years ending in 1997.

If the rest of the country reacted as did Floridian permit holders, the United States would have the lowest homicide rate in the world!

The gun-banners say that if you try to use a gun to protect yourself from an attacker, the attacker will take it away from you and use it on you. They say you're better off to offer no resistance, or to do as they say and let them rob you or rape you.

Kleck says, "Victims [who defended themselves with a firearm] were less likely to report being injured than those who either defended themselves by other means or took no self-protective measures at all. Thus, while 33 percent of all surviving robbery victims were injured, only 25 percent of those who offered no resistance and 17 percent of those who defended themselves with guns were injured." He also states that only one percent of gun defenders lost a gun to the criminal.

The gun-banners would have you believe that if you own a gun you are most likely to shoot a family member or someone you know in the course of defensive gun use.

Kleck says this kind of shooting is extremely rare. Less than two percent of fatal gun accidents occur during defensive gun use. Out of 1,500 fatal gun accidents a year, that amounts to 30 a year. Consider that out of two million defensive gun uses per year, the odds against such a thing happening are about 1 in 65,000.

Professors James Wright and Peter Rossi, authors of *Armed and Considered Dangerous: A Survey of Felons and Their Firearms*, surveyed 2,000 felons in state prisons across the country, and said that 34 percent said they had been "scared off, shot at, wounded, or captured by armed citizens." Nearly 70 percent said that they knew at least one other criminal who had, also. Another third said that when they were thinking about committing a crime they worried that their intended victim might shoot them.

As I stated earlier, most criminals are more concerned about getting shot than about getting caught by the police. That knowledge comes from my own experience, working with them in Oregon prisons for twenty years.

One liberal "expert," Arthur Kellerman, claims in an article in the *New England Journal of Medicine*, that a homeowner's gun is 43 times more likely to kill a family member than an intruder. Kleck says this is a "nonsense ratio." Kellerman says, "For every case of self-protection homicide involving a firearm kept in the home, there are 1.3 accidental deaths, 4.6 criminal homicides, and 37 suicides involving firearms." The statement has been quoted over and over again in medical journals, government publications and non-technical newsletters, etc., as well as in letters-to-the-editor and in Op-Ed pieces.

Kellerman's methodology has been exposed as not only seriously flawed, but also using the same approach for violent deaths in the home not involving firearms the risk factor more than doubles, from 43 to 1, to 99 to 1. He bases his figures only from gunshot deaths in King County, Washington.

Yet, for those who already have their minds made up—the liberal media and the gun-grabbers—his figures are eagerly seized upon and disseminated.

Semi-automatic firearms that look like military weapons but do not differ materially from any other semi-automatic firearm—some of which have been around for more than a century—are characterized by the anti-firearms media and politicians as "assault weapons." The thing to remember is that they are not assault weapons. They cannot fire on full automatic. They only fire one bullet with each pull of the trigger, which is exactly the same thing a double-action revolver does. Furthermore, they are usually less powerful than other such firearms, although the media nearly always refers to them as "high-powered rifles."

The infamous AK-47 we have heard so much about fires an anemic 7.65 X 39mm cartridge, which has roughly the same ballistics as the old Winchester Model of 1894 .30-30 lever action rifle. The Winchester is usually considered effective to about 100 yards, whereas the .30-'06 (for which the Second World War military rifle, the M-1 Garand was chambered) is effective up to 1,000 yards.

The AR-15, which the Washington, D.C., sniper of recent infamy used, is chambered for the .223 cartridge. The AR-15 is the civilian version of the M-16 military rifle. The .223 is a hot .22 caliber. It is illegal to hunt deer with it in most states because it is more likely to wound the animal and cause a slow death than to give a quick kill. The military prefer a weapon that wounds, rather than one that kills instantly, because it takes out not only the target but also removes the men from the field that must carry him out.

These so-called assault weapons have never been the first choice of criminals. They are only used in about a fifth of one percent of all violent crimes, and rifles of any type are rarely used in suicides—between three and four percent. So, what's the big objection to them?

The anti-gunners seek to outlaw firearms one type at a time, one step at a time, until they eventually outlaw them all. It would do well to remember the words of the Reverend Martin Niemöller, who lived in Nazi Germany:

> *"First they came for the Jews. I was silent. I was not a Jew. Then they came for the Communists. I was silent. I was not a Communist. Then they came for the trade unionists. I was silent. I was not a trade unionist. Then they came for me. There was no one left to speak for me."*

I don't own an AR-15, nor a semi-automatic knock-off of an AK-47. I don't buy what I consider to be ugly guns. But that does not mean that I will condone any prohibition of either of them, nor of a "Saturday night special," nor "cop-killer bullets," nor "sniper rifles" when they finally get around to bolt-action rifles with scope sights.

Personally, I think that any law-abiding citizen should be allowed to legally own full automatic weapons—including "Tommy guns"—just as long as our employees, the police, have them. In fact, any hand-held firearm that our government—either the military or the police—are equipped with should be lawfully available to the militia, and I am a member of the militia.

Who are they afraid of?

Why should the citizenry, who have the final responsibility for keeping the peace and directing the government, not be as well armed as their servants?

I personally do not want such weapons, but nevertheless it should be my right to own them, and to own them without filling out any government questionnaires or forms, or providing them any information, including "fingerprinting" the firearm, or registering it, or providing any other information to any bureaucrat to exercise that right. Registration is virtually always the precursor to confiscation, and the bully-boys virtually always follow confiscation of the means of self-protection. It is the nature of government, universally, to grow more powerful, and power of course means power over the people by an armed elite. As Mao Tse-tung observed, "Our principle is that the Party commands the gun, and the gun must never be allowed to command the Party."

An armed populace necessarily diminishes the potential for absolute power. I do not understand those who would readily give up their freedom for the false promise of imaginary security. Freedom is the universally desired state of all individuals, and security is an illusion. It can never truly exist because there are too many unknown factors in a dynamic universe. All the risks can never be known and protected against. Better to recognize that and prepare to defend yourself as much as possible.

11

More About Firearms

In this chapter we will discuss some of the details of various firearms, and introduce the reader to the niceties of taking them apart for cleaning, etc.

First let us take a look at the old Government model of 1911, the Colt semi-automatic pistol. To fieldstrip the pistol for cleaning and maintenance, perform the following steps:

1. Hold the pistol in the raised pistol position and press the button on the left side, releasing the magazine.

2. Inspect the chamber to ascertain that there is no cartridge in it.

3. Press down on the recoil spring plug and turn the barrel bushing a quarter turn clockwise, and allow the recoil spring to expand slowly and remove the plug. Leave the recoil spring in place. (See the picture below for nomenclature of the various parts of the pistol).

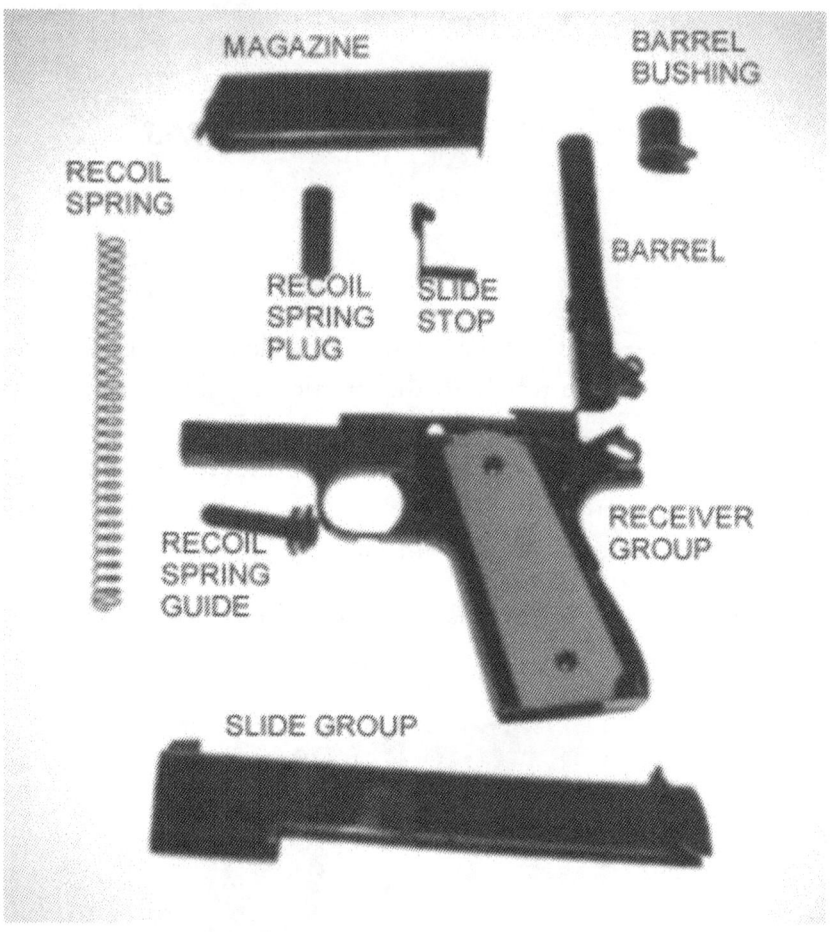

4. Press the thumb safety lock down to the "fire" position. Push the slide to the rear till the disassembly notch is lined up with the rear projection on the slide stop, then press the slide stop projection on the right side of the pistol and remove the slide stop.

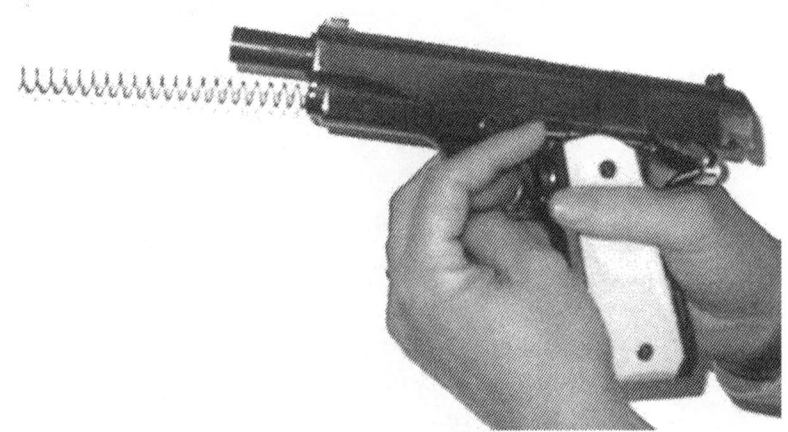

5. Pull the receiver back to separate it from the slide as shown in the next photo, and remove the recoil spring and guide, and the barrel bushing from the slide.

6. Remove the barrel from the slide and remove the recoil spring guide and the recoil spring. Separate them with a twisting action.

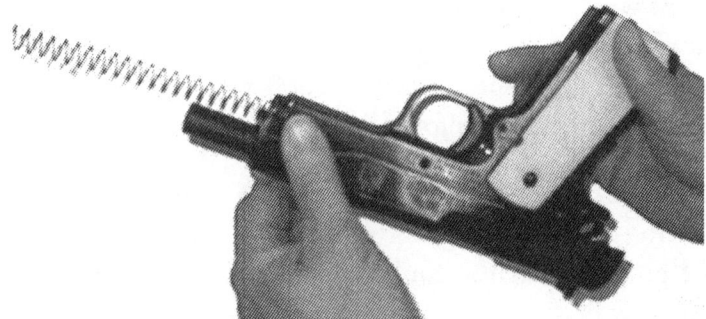

7. Remove the barrel bushing by turning it counter-clockwise and pulling it from the slide and remove the barrel as shown.

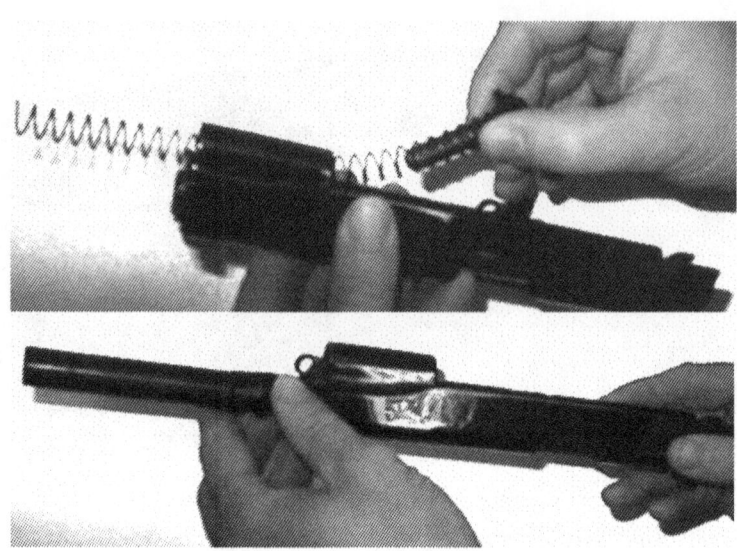

To reassemble the pistol, reverse the directions above.

The Colt .45 ACP semi-auto is widely cloned, and the takedown procedures outlined above are typical of many semi-autos, with some notable variations. Usually, if you purchase a new gun, the takedown directions will be included in the owner's manual, along with the safety rules for handling the firearm.

Cleaning implements and other tools you should have with you in your gun box include the following:

1. A set of screwdrivers that fit the screws on your firearm exactly—preferably hollow ground ones. You don't want to deface the grooves on your gun's screws. The screwdrivers are useful to adjust your sights, among other uses, if your pistol or revolver is equipped with adjustable sights.

2. Cans of gun oil and powder solvent.

3. Bore brushes in the appropriate size, preferably in stainless steel.

4. Cotton patches in the appropriate size for the caliber firearm you are using. (They can be made of old T-shirts, or any lint free white soft cotton cloth.)

5. A bore swab of the appropriate size, as well as a pistol cleaning rod and tips.

6. A couple of toothbrushes for cleaning the corners and hidden areas.

The other items you will need when you go shooting will of course be ammunition, targets, thumbtacks or a stapler to fasten the targets to the frame, or stump, or whatever they will be fastened to. You will come up with other items that you will find handy as you go along, like a shooting mat to lie on for prone shooting, and other accouterments.

It is not necessary to pay for a fancy shooting box. You might well start with an inexpensive plastic fishing tackle box that is large enough to hold everything.

Don't forget the shooting glasses and ear protection!

Cleaning a revolver is simpler. You can simply swing the cylinder out, using the thumb latch on the left side of the gun. You will notice that the latch varies with the manufacturer; for example, the Colt typically has one that looks like this:

With the Colt revolver, the thumb release is drawn back with the thumb, which releases the cylinder to roll out of the frame to the left, enabling you to clean both the cylinder and the barrel.

With the Smith & Wesson, it is the opposite. The thumb release is pushed forward with the thumb, releasing the cylinder. The same is true with the Brazilian made Taurus revolvers and the Charter Arms "Bulldog" which we saw earlier.

Note also that the small arrowhead notches in the side of the cylinders on both the Colt and the S&W revolvers, clearly visible in the photo below, point in the direction that the cylinder revolves, which differs on the Colt and S&W guns. On the Colt, the cylinder revolves clockwise, looking from the shooter's viewpoint, while on the S&W the cylinder rotates counter-clockwise.

The cleaning of the two weapons proceeds in the same manner for each, and for all other makes and models as well.

It is of primary importance that the barrel be free of lead particles. If the firearm is not cleaned after every outing, the lead particles will build up in the lands and grooves of the rifling, shown below:

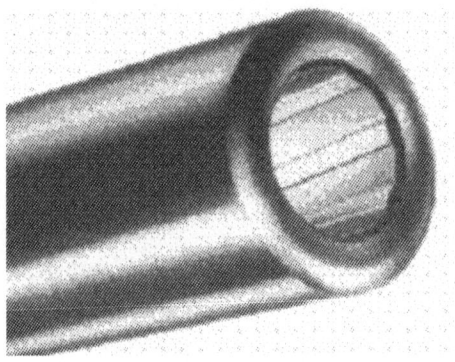

The buildup of lead can cause serious damage to the weapon if it is not removed entirely, as each time the gun is fired with a dirty barrel, the buildup increases, and it will not be expelled by a jacketed bullet. It can cause a bulge in the barrel in extreme cases. Remove it with your bore brush after each shooting expedition. Of course the phenomenon is worse if you shoot primarily unjacketed lead bullets, in which case you must be particularly careful. My late friend, George Tooley, who taught policemen and correctional officers to shoot for decades, and was himself a pistol master, used a piece of brazing rod with one end sharpened and bent at about a 5-degree angle in one end and at right angles on the other, which he used to remove stubborn lead buildup from his guns. He fired a lot of cast lead bullets. They are considerably cheaper than the store-bought jacketed stuff.

Many regular shooters reload their ammunition, not only because it is cheaper, but also because they can control their loads. However, that is a subject for another book, and many books and manuals are on the market that cover the subject to exhaustion.

To examine the bore of your revolver you may want to invest in a bore light, shown below.

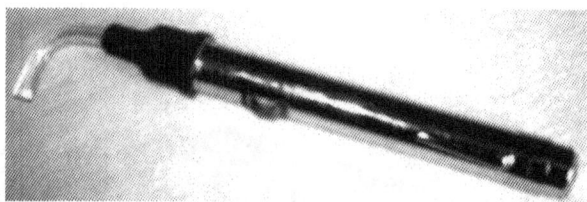

It is a neat little device with which you can see into the barrel of your pistol or revolver clearly. Stick the light into the frame end of the firearm and look into the muzzle. The bore will be well lighted and you can easily detect any obstructions or lead buildup. If you don't want to expend the money to buy one (they are inexpensive) or can't find one, simply place a white piece of paper in the frame opening after the cylinder is swung out, to reflect the light, and look into the muzzle.

Cleaning your firearm is important, and should be done with care. On a revolver, it is not necessary to take off the side plates or get into the internal guts of the instrument. You are better off to leave it alone unless you are knowledgeable and skilled at firearms repair. Every gunsmith has experienced the gunner who has dismantled his gun, can't get it back together again and ends up taking it to the gunsmith in a box for reassembly. Embarrassing!

Revolvers are generally fitted so tightly that no dust or dirt can get inside, anyway. The places to be concerned with are the cylinder (including the ends), barrel, forcing cone (the end of the barrel nearest the cylinder, which is cone shaped), and the pressure plate (the dome shaped area directly behind the cylinder). Clean those areas well with your stainless steel or brass bore brush, soaked in powder solvent. Scrub the dirty areas well, but use a toothbrush on the blued surfaces, as the metal brush will scratch bluing. Then, wipe the cleaned areas with soft, lint free cloth, and run white patches through the barrel until they come out clean. After cleaning, put a *few drops* of gun oil on your bore swab and run it through the bore with a twisting motion. Do not expose your cartridges to gun oil, as it can penetrate around the primer and render the cartridge useless. *Do not over lubricate!*

The procedure is about the same for cleaning a semi-automatic, with obvious differences due to the dissimilarity of construction. The automatic needs to be taken apart more thoroughly for cleaning, as discussed earlier. It is very important, though to refrain from over lubricating. Just a couple of drops on the slide rails and moving parts, and then wipe the gun clean with a dry, soft cloth.

Shooting is generally done at targets, or bowling pins, or falling plates, depending on the kind of sport or practice you are interested in. There are many formal competitions you might wish to engage in, from bullseye competition, to IPSC action shooting, or perhaps you'd like to take part in the events put on by the Single Action Shooting Society.

And then there is the good old tin can! That kind of shooting is called "plinking", and it can be a lot of fun on a weekend in the woods or at the gravel pit. But, remember to check your backdrop! Remember that you are firing a projectile that can cause considerable damage. Don't shoot into the trees unless you are positive that there is no one back there, and no animals that might be injured or killed.

One last "don't." Don't shoot or handle firearms when you have been drinking. Gunpowder and alcohol don't mix well.

It is my hope that this book will be of use to you, and help to increase your shooting pleasure as well as encourage some reflection on the importance of an armed populace, and what it means to maintaining our freedom.

Freemen are armed. Slaves are disarmed.

Selected Quotations

The following are some quotations from people down through the centuries regarding the right and necessity of the people to arm themselves.

"Armaque in armatos sumere iura sinunt"
("The laws allow arms to be taken against an armed foe")

—Ovid

"We are all of us carried along by a fiery zeal to recover our liberty; our arms cannot be wrested from our hands."

—Cicero
Philippics (42 B.C.)

"As Aristotle tells us, in his fourth book on Politics, the Grecian states ever had special care to place the use and exercise of arms in the people, because the commonwealth is theirs who hold the arms: the sword and sovereignty ever walk hand in hand together."

—Marchamont Nedham
The Right Constitution of a Commonwealth (1656)

"It is not reasonable to suppose that one who is armed will obey willingly one who is unarmed; or that an unarmed man will remain safe among armed servants."

"…For men who are well disciplined will always be cautious of violating the laws when they have arms in their hands as when they have not…"

—Machiavelli
The Prince

The "summe of the Right of Nature" is "by all means we can to defend our selves." "A man cannot lay down the right of resisting them, that assault him by force, to take away his life…"

"Covenants without the Sword are but Words, and of no strength to secure a man at all."

—Thomas Hobbes
Leviathan (1651)

"The distribution of arms among her citizens prevents a monarch from overcoming a republic."

—James Harrington
Oceana (1688)

"The possession of arms is the distinction between a freeman and a slave. He who has nothing, and belongs to another, must be defended by him, and needs no arms: but he who thinks he is his own master, and has anything he may call his own, ought to have arms to defend himself and what he possesses, or else he lives precariously and at discretion. And though for a while those who have the sword in their power abstain from doing him injury; yet, by degrees, he will be awed into submission to every arbitrary command. Our ancestors, by being always armed, and frequently in action, defended themselves against the Romans, Danes and English; and maintained their liberty against encroachments of their own princes."

—Andrew Fletcher (1673)
Scottish Whig

"Our Armies formerly were only a Number of the People armed occasionally; and Armies of the People are the only Armies which are not formidable to the People."
"When a tyrant's Army is beaten, his Country is conquered: He has no Resource; his Subjects having neither Arms nor Courage, nor Reason to fight for him..." but, "in Attacks upon a free State, every Man has something to defend in it."
"The Exercise of despotic Power is the unrelenting War of an armed Tyrant Upon his unarmed Subjects."

—John Trenchard and Thomas Gordon
Cato's Letters (1721-22)

"False is the idea of utility that sacrifices a thousand real advantages for one imaginary or trifling inconvenience; that would take fire from men because it burns, and water because one may drown in it; that has no remedy for evils, except destruction. The laws that forbid the carrying of arms are laws of such a nature. They disarm those who are neither inclined nor determined to commit crimes. Can it be supposed that those who have the courage to violate the most sacred laws of humanity, the most important of the code, will respect the less important and arbitrary ones, which can be violated with ease and impunity, and which, if strictly observed, would put an end to personal liberty—so dear to men, so dear to the enlightened legislator—and subject innocent persons to all the vexations that the guilty alone ought to suffer? Such laws make things worse for the assaulted and better for the assailants; they serve rather to encourage than to prevent homicides, for an unarmed man may be attacked with greater confidence than an armed man. They ought to be designated as laws not preventive but fearful of crimes, produced by the tumultuous impression of a few isolated facts, and not by thoughtful consideration of the inconveniences and advantages of a universal decree."

—Cesare Beccaria
On Crimes and Punishment (1764)

"Instances of the licentious and outrageous behavior of the military conservators of the peace still multiply among us, some of which are of such nature, and have been carried to such great lengths, as must serve fully to evince that a late vote of this town, calling upon all inhabitants to provide themselves with arms for their defence, was a measure as prudent as it was legal...it is a natural right which the people have reserved to themselves, confirmed by the [English] Bill of Rights, to keep arms for their own defence; and as Mr. Blackstone observes, it is to be made use of when the sanctions of society and law are found insufficient to restrain the violence of oppression."

—*A Journal of the Times* (1768-69)
Boston

"A well regulated Militia, composed of gentlemen, freeholders, and other freemen, is the natural strength and stable security of a free Government."

—New Castle County (Delaware) Committee (1775)

"...recommended to such of the inhabitants of this County as are from sixteen to fifty years of age that they provide themselves with good Firelocks..."

"And we do each of us, for ourselves respectively, promise and engage to keep a good Fire-lock in proper Order & to furnish Ourselves as soon as possible with, & always keep by us, one Pound of Gunpowder, four Pounds of lead, one Dozen Gun-flints, & a pair of Bullet-Moulds, with a Cartouch Box, or powder-horn, and Bag for Balls."

—George Mason, Fairfax County (Virginia) Committee (1775)

"It is always dangerous to the liberties of the people to have an army stationed among them, over which they have no control."
"The militia is composed of free Citizens. There is therefore no Danger of their making use of their Power, to the destruction of their own Rights, or suffering others to invade them."

—Samuel Adams (1775)

"That a well regulated militia, composed of gentlemen and yeomen [landowners], is the natural strength and only security of a free government."
"They tell us that we are weak—unable to cope with so formidable an adversary. But when shall we be stronger?...Will it be when we are totally disarmed, and when a British guard shall be stationed in every house?...Three million people, armed in the holy cause of liberty are invincible by any force which our enemy can send against us."
"The great object is, that every man be armed..."
"guard with jealous attention the public liberty. Suspect every one who approaches that jewel. Unfortunately, nothing will preserve it but downright force. Whenever you give up that force, you are ruined."
"Are we at last brought to such a humiliating and debasing degradation, that we cannot be trusted with arms for our own defense? Where is the difference between having arms in our own possession and under our own direction, and having them under the management of Con-

gress? If our defense be the *real* object of having those arms, in whose hands can they be trusted with more propriety, or equal safety to us, as in our *own* hands?"

"Gentlemen may cry, peace, peace—but there is no peace. The war is actually begun! The next gale that sweeps from the north will bring to our ears the clash of resounding arms! Our brethren are already in the field! Why stand we here idle? What is it that gentlemen wish? What would they have? Is life so dear, or peace so sweet, as to be purchased at the price of chains and slavery? Forbid it, Almighty God! I know not what course others may take; but as for me, give me liberty, or give me death."

—Patrick Henry

"…to disarm the people; that it was the best and most effectual way to enslave them…by totally disusing and neglecting the militia."

"Who are the militia? They consist of the whole people, except a few public officers."

—George Mason

"A militia, when properly formed, are in fact the people themselves, and render regular troops in great measure unnecessary…The Constitution ought to secure a genuine militia and guard against a select militia, by providing that the militia shall always be kept well organized, armed and disciplined, and include all men capable of bearing arms; and that all regulations tending to render this general militia useless and defenseless, by establishing select corps of militia, or distinct bodies of military men, not having permanent interests and attachments in the community to be avoided."

—Richard Henry Lee
Letters from the Federal Farmer (1788)

"Congress may give us a select militia [National Guard] which will, in fact, be a standing army—or Congress, afraid of a general militia, may say there shall be no militia at all.
"When a select militia is formed; the people in general may be disarmed."

—John Smilie
In the Pennsylvania Convention

"None but an armed nation can dispense with a standing army. To keep ours armed and disciplined is therefore at all times important."
"We cannot be defended but by making every citizen a soldier, as the Greeks and Romans who had no standing armies."
"God forbid we should ever be twenty years without such a rebellion...And what country can preserve its liberties, if its rulers are not warned from time to time, that this people preserve the spirit of resistance? Let them take arms...The tree of liberty must be refreshed from time to time, with the blood of patriots and tyrants." (1787)

—Thomas Jefferson

"Before a standing army can rule, the people must be disarmed; as they are in almost every kingdom in Europe. The supreme power in America cannot enforce unjust laws by the sword; because the whole body of the people are armed, and constitute a force superior to any band of regular troops that can be, on any pretence, raised in the United States. A military force, at the command of Congress, can execute no laws, but such as the people perceive to be just and constitutional; for they will possess the power, and jealousy will instantly inspire the inclination, to resist the execution of a law which appears to them unjust and oppressive."

—Noah Webster

"If the representatives of the people betray their constituents, there is then no recourse left but the exertion of that original right of self-defense which is paramount to all positive forms of government…"

—Alexander Hamilton
The Federalist No. 28

"…The ultimate authority…resides in the people alone"
To a regular army of the United States government "would be opposed a militia amounting to near a half a million citizens with arms in their hands" Referring to "the advantage of being armed, which the Americans possess over the people of almost every other nation."

—James Madison
The Federalist No. 4

"These are the times that try men's souls: The summer soldier and the sunshine patriot will, in this crisis, shrink from the service of his country; but he that stands it NOW, deserves the love and thanks of man and woman. Tyranny, like hell, is not easily conquered; yet we have this consolation with us, that the harder the conflict, the more glorious the triumph. What we obtain too cheap, we esteem too lightly: 'Tis dearness only that gives every thing its value. Heaven knows how to put a proper price upon its goods; and it would be strange indeed, if so celestial an article as FREEDOM should not be highly rated. Britain, with an army to enforce her tyranny, has declared that she has the right (not only to TAX) but "to BIND us in ALL CASES WHATSOEVER," and if being bound in that manner, is not slavery, then there is not such a thing as slavery upon earth. Even the expression is impious, for so unlimited a power can belong only to GOD."

—Thomas Paine
Crisis

"So if a law be in opposition to the Constitution; if both the law and the Constitution apply to a particular case, so that the court must either decide that case conformably to the law, disregarding the Constitution; or conformably to the Constitution, disregarding the law; the court must determine which of these conflicting rules governs the case. This is the very essence of judicial duty.

"If, then, the courts are to regard the Constitution, and the Constitution is superior to any ordinary act of the legislature, the Constitution, and not such an ordinary act, must govern the case to which they both apply...

"Thus, the particular phraseology of the Constitution of the United States confirms and strengthens the principle, supposed to be essential to all written constitutions, that a law repugnant to the Constitution is void; and that courts, as well as other departments, are bound by that instrument."

—John Marshall
Chief Justice, United States Supreme Court
Marbury vs. Madison (1803)

Handgun Glossary

Action: The working parts of a handgun, whether a single shot, revolver, semi-automatic, derringer or sub-machine pistol.

Ammunition: The cartridge fired in a handgun, composed of the case, propellant (gunpowder), primer and the bullet. Often erroneously referred to by the press simply as "bullets."

Armor-Piercing: Ammunition in which the bullet is composed of any of several metals harder than lead, and usually coated with Teflon or nylon.

Assault Weapon: Originally an "assault rifle" was a term derived from the German sturmgewehr, which translates to "storm rifle", a weapon capable of being fired either as a semi-automatic (one shot fired with each pull of the trigger), a short burst with each pull of the trigger, or full-automatic (fires continuously as long as the trigger is held down). Nearly always less powerful than a battle rifle. The term has lately been used indiscriminately by the press to include handguns (particularly semi-automatics).

Automatic Pistol: A true automatic pistol is one which can fire full-automatic; that is, continuously as long as the trigger is held down. The term is commonly use, however to describe semi-automatic pistols, which fire only one round with each pull of the trigger.

Barrel: The cylinder through which the bullet passes when the cartridge is fired. It may be smooth, as in a shotgun, or rifled with spiraling lands and grooves, designed to give the bullet a spin.

Battery: Before a firearm can be fired a cartridge must be inserted into firing position in the chamber, where the firing pin may strike the primer upon pulling the trigger. This is called "bringing it into battery."

Bench rest: A table or shooting station designed to eliminate movement of a firearm while it is being fired. Also a type of competition shooting requiring great accuracy of both the firearm and the shooter.

Blackpowder: The original propellant used in firearms, which originated in China in prehistorical times. Except for aficionados of blackpowder shooting, utilizing replicas of antique firearms, it has been almost universally replaced with smokeless powder.

Blank Cartridge: A cartridge that has no projectile and usually only a light powder charge, usually used in movies and in starter pistols. Although they do not have a projectile, they are still dangerous at short range.

Bore: The inside of the barrel of a firearm, whether rifled or not. If the firearm has no rifling, it is often referred to as a "smoothbore."

Brass: The metallic case of a cartridge, which holds the propellant (gunpowder) and into which the bullet and the primer are inserted.

Bullet: The projectile component of the cartridge, which may be constructed of solid lead or any number of alloys, and may or may not be coated. The term is not synonymous with the complete cartridge, although it is often so referred to by uninformed news people and others.

Caliber: Usually refers to the diameter of a bullet or the diameter between the lands of rifling in the barrel of a firearm, and in the United States it is usually expressed in decimal parts of an inch, while elsewhere it may be expressed in millimeters.

Carbine: A rifle with a shorter than average barrel, usually more than 16 (by law) and up to 20 inches. Originally developed for use by cavalry soldiers.

Cartridge: A round of ammunition, composed of a case, primer, bullet, and propellant.

Case: One of the components of a cartridge, and usually the most expensive part, which may be reloaded and used again by hand loaders.

Center-fire: A cartridge which has the primer (explosive device) inserted in the center of the base. Also refers to a firearm that utilizes such a cartridge.

Chamber: the end of the barrel, which is screwed into the receiver of a firearm, as opposed to the muzzle, and into which the cartridge is inserted when the gun is brought into battery.

Clip: A metallic device, which holds a stack of cartridges and may be used to insert them into the breach of a rifle. Usually the clip is ejected from the rifle automatically. The term is often erroneously used to describe a magazine, which is either a fixed or detachable object used to hold cartridges that becomes a functional part of a handgun or rifle.

Cylinder: The rotating part of a revolver which holds the cartridges, and brings each into battery when the hammer is cocked, or the trigger is pulled—depending on whether the piece is to be fired single or double action.

Derringer: A usually small pistol with one or more barrels—most often two—with a single round loaded into each barrel.

Detonate: An explosion, as when the primer of a cartridge is struck by the firing pin. The detonation ignites the smokeless powder in the case, which burns rapidly, creating gas that then propels the bullet out of the cartridge and down the barrel.

Double-action: When the trigger is used to retract the hammer, which revolves the cylinder bringing a cartridge into battery. When the trigger reaches the point where the sear releases the hammer, it causes the firing pin to strike the cartridge's primer and fire the projectile. Also the description of a revolver that may be used to fire either single action or double action.

Double-action only (DAO): The description of either a revolver or semi-automatic pistol, which may be fired only in the double-action mode.

Expanding bullet: A projectile designed to expand on impact, either because it is a hollow-point, or because it is of a frangible design.

Firearm: A handgun or long gun (rifle or shotgun) either with or without rifling in the barrel, which uses gunpowder as a propellant.

Firing Pin: A spring-loaded pin in the receiver section of a firearm that is released by the trigger mechanism, striking the cartridge primer which ignites the gunpowder in the cartridge case, resulting in the bullet being driven down the barrel by the resultant gasses.

Full metal jacket: A term applied to a bullet that is completely covered by a hard metal jacket. FMJs do not expand on impact, and leave little or no residue in the barrel of the firearm.

Frangible bullet: A bullet, or projectile, that is designed to separate into small fragments on impact.

Gauge: Not applicable to handguns. The measure of a shotgun barrel's diameter, expressed in the number of lead pellets it requires of that diameter to equal one pound.

Grip safety: Found on semi-automatic pistols, it is a device that prevents the pistol from firing unless the handle is gripped firmly.

Gun: A term commonly used in the United States that is synonymous with the word firearm. Elsewhere (in England, for example) it refers only to the shotgun.

Gunpowder: A composition of various chemicals in differing particle shapes and sizes, the purpose of which is to act as a propellant in cartridges. The various combinations burn at different rates, and provide differing effects in terms of muzzle velocity of the projectile. There are two basic types of gunpowder: blackpowder and smokeless powder. The latter burns with very little smoke, and the former with considerable emission of white smoke.

Half jacket: A bullet that is half-jacketed with hard metal, the other half of which is not coated.

Handgun: A firearm, which is designed to be handheld, i.e.: a revolver, semi-automatic pistol or a single or multi-barreled handheld gun.

Hollow-point bullet: A bullet with a concave opening on the presenting end, enabling it to expand when it strikes a target.

Jacket: The metallic case coating some bullets, often made of copper or some other similar metal which has the effect of hardening the bullet and preventing loss of the bullet material and therefore changing its shape as it passes down the barrel.

Machine gun: A full-automatic firearm, or one with selective fire, either a rifle or pistol, which continuously fires at a rapid rate as long as the trigger is held down, or can be fired semi-automatically or in the burst mode at the shooter's discretion.

Magazine: A device to hold several rounds of ammunition, spring loaded so that it feeds each round in turn into the firing chamber, enabling the shooter to fire successively with each pull of the trigger. When inserted into the firearm, it becomes an integral part of the firearm, as opposed to a clip, which is ejected automatically when empty, or a stripper clip that releases the cartridges it carries into the receiver and then is withdrawn.

Magnum: A cartridge that is loaded with a heavier than normal powder charge for a particular caliber. The term originated with the large sized bottle of champagne.

Muzzle: the front opening on the barrel of a gun from which the bullet exits.

Muzzle blast: The explosive release of gas from the muzzle when the bullet exits the barrel. It results in a load report and a flash of flame from the muzzle, accompanied by recoil.

Muzzle brake: An attachment on the muzzle of a gun the purpose of which is to divert the gasses produced when the gun is fired to cut down on recoil and muzzle blast.

Pistol: Another word for handgun, sometimes used to specifically denote a semi-automatic, but it also is appropriate to use it to refer to revolvers.

Pistol grip: The handle, or scales, on the butt of a pistol, usually made of wood, plastic, ivory, metal or rubber and attached to the frame with screws.

Plinking: A popular pastime with firearms. An informal type of shooting using a variety of targets, i.e. tin cans, bottles, garbage, etc., often in the forest or a gravel pit.

Point: The tip of the bullet.

Powder: Gunpowder.

Primer: The explosive component of a cartridge, composed usually of fulminate of mercury or lead styphnate, which is activated when the firing pin strikes it, resulting in the ignition of the powder charge in the cartridge.

Projectile: A bullet.

Propellant: The gunpowder component of a cartridge, which, ignited by the primer, burns rapidly, giving off gasses that propel the bullet down the barrel of a gun.

Pyrodex: A modern substitute for black powder, safer to handle than black powder, which is explosive.

Receiver: The breech housing, enclosing the firing pin, trigger mechanism, the chamber of a firearm and related mechanisms.

Recoil: The sometimes disconcerting jump, or kick, of a pistol resulting from the explosive release of gasses and the expulsion of the bullet from the barrel, following the Third Law of Motion: For every action, there is an equal and opposite reaction.

Revolver: A handgun, usually, although Colt Firearms also built rifles with revolving cylinders. The revolving cylinder into which the cartridges are loaded typifies these firearms. The revolution of the cylinder caused either by pulling the trigger or pulling the hammer back brings a cartridge into battery and fires it when the trigger pull is completed. In operation, it has the same result as a semi-automatic pistol, firing each time the trigger is pulled. Only the mechanism to accomplish that is different.

Rifling: Spiral lands and grooves in the gun's barrel, which impart a spin to the bullet as it travels down the barrel, thus assisting to stabilize it in its flight to the target.

Rimfire: As opposed to centerfire, qv. The best known are the various .22 caliber cartridges, although in the past other larger calibers have also been rimfires. In the rimfire cartridge, the primer is located in the outer flanged rim at the base of the cartridge, rather than in the center of the base, as with the center fire.

Round: The expression normally used to describe a single cartridge of ammunition.

Sabot: A method of firing a small caliber bullet through a gun otherwise chambered for a larger caliber, through the mechanism of a lightweight carrier.

Saturday Night Special: There is no such animal! This a propaganda phrase initiated by the press to indicate inexpensive handguns. There is no legal or practical definition except in their fevered imaginations.

Scope: A telescopic sight used by some pistoleers on their handguns, especially for hunting.

Sear: That portion of the trigger mechanism that mechanically releases the bolt or firing pin.

Selective fire: A switch on a firearm allowing it, at the discretion of the shooter, to fire on full automatic, semi-automatic, or in a short burst. A $200 license fee must be paid in order to have lawful ownership of such a weapon unless the user is in the police or military.

Semi-automatic: These pistols fire a single cartridge each time the trigger is pulled, the same as does a double action revolver. The primary difference is that the semi-auto ejects the fired cartridge and loads another. The revolver fires until it is empty, but then must be manually reloaded. The mechanisms are different, but the result is about the same.

Semi-wadcutter: A bullet with a blunt nose, but not as blunt as a wadcutter.

Sight: Any device used to aim a firearm.

Sighting in: The act of zeroing the firearm in so that the point of impact of the bullet agrees with the sight picture at some particular range.

Silencer: The technical term is "suppressor" but they are often referred to as a silencer. The mechanism reduces, but does not silence the report of a pistol. They are virtually illegal to possess, for no good reason.

Single-action: Any firearm in which the hammer must be manually cocked before the trigger can be used to fire the round.

Single-shot: A firearm that requires each cartridge to be loaded manually for each shot fired, just as the name implies.

Snub-nose: A pistol with a short barrel, usually used to describe a revolver with a barrel of about 2-inches.

Spotting Scope: A high-powered telescope used to spot the effect of a round fired on a target. Used with a tripod.

Striker: The firing pin, which strikes the primer.

Submachine gun: A full automatic firearm that fires continuously at a rapid rate as long as the trigger is held down, usually firing pistol ammunition of .45 ACP or 9mm caliber.

Teflon: The name of a synthetic plastic coating used on jacketed bullets to protect the rifling. The press has made such bullets infamous, calling them "cop killer" bullets, although no policeman has ever been killed by such a projectile piercing his body armor.

Trajectory: The curved path a bullet takes to the target.

Trigger: The finger operated mechanism operated by the shooter to fire a round. Also, the name of Roy Roger's horse.

Twist: The rate at which the bullet revolves in the barrel as the result of the spiral lands and grooves.

Wadcutter: A cast pistol bullet of a blunt shape used primarily for target shooting.

Bibliography

AYOOB, Massad, *In the Gravest Extreme Role of the Firearm*, Police Bookshelf, 1980
—*The Ayoob Files*, Police Bookshelf, 1995
—*The Truth About Self Protection*, Police Bookshelf, 1985

BASS, Dr. Joseph L, *A Little Handbook on the Second Amendment: What the American Aristocracy Does Not Want You to Know*, The Downtown Enterprise, 1999

BRANCA, Andrew F., *The Law of Self Defense: A Guide for the Armed Citizen*, Operon Security, Ltd., 1998

CLEDE, Bill, *The Practical Pistol Manual: How to Use a Handgun for Self-Defense*, Jameson Books, 1997

COOPER, Jeff, *To Ride, Shoot Straight, And Speak The Truth*, Paladin Press, 1998

GOTTLIEB, Alan, *Gun Rights Fact Book*, Merril Press, 1988

HALBROOK, Stephen, *That Every Man Be Armed: The Evolution of a Constitutional Right*, Independent Inst., 1994
—*Freedmen, the Fourteenth Amendment, and the Right to Bear Arms, 1866-1876*, Praeger Pub, 1998
—*A Right to Bear Arms: State and Federal Bills of Rights and Constitutional Guarantees (Contributions in Political Science)*, Greenwood Publishing Group

HOROWITZ, David, and POE, David, *The Seven Myths of Gun Control: Reclaiming the Truth About Guns, Crime, and the Second Amendment*, Prima Publishing, 2001

KLECK, Dr. Gary, *Point Blank: Guns and Violence in America (Social Institutions and Social Change)*, Aldine de Gruyter, 1991
—*Targeting Guns: Firearms and Their Control (Social Institutions and Social Change)*, Aldine de Gruyter, 1997

KOPEL, David, *The Samurai, the Mountie, and the Cowboy: Should America Adopt the Gun Controls of Other Democracies,* Prometheus Books, 1992
—*No More Wacos: What's Wrong With Federal Law Enforcement and How to Fix It,* Prometheus Books, 1997
—*Guns, Who Should Have Them?* Prometheus Books, 1995
—*Gun Control in Great Britain: Saving Lives or Constricting Liberties?* Office of International Criminal Justice, 1992

LOTT, Dr. John, *More Guns, Less Crime: Understanding Crime and Gun-Control Laws(Studies in Law and Economics),* University of Chicago Press, 2000

MALCOLM, Joyce Lee, *To Keep and Bear Arms: The Origins of an Anglo-American Right,* Harvard University Press, 1996
—*Guns and Violence: The English Experience,* Harvard University Press, 2002

McCLURG, Andrew J., *Gun Control and Gun Rights: A Reader and Guide,* New York University Press, 2002

QUIGLEY, Paxton, *Armed & Female,* St. Martin's, 1994
—*Not an Easy Target: Paxton Quigley's Self-Protection for Women,* Fireside, 1995

TOOLEY, George L., *George Tooley's Beginner's Book on How to Handle Firearms Safely,* iUniverse, 2000

WATERS, Robert, *The Best Defense: True Stories of Intended Victims Who Defended Themselves With a Firearm,* Cumberland House, 1998

U.S. SENATE Judiciary Committee, *The Right to Keep and Bear Arms, Senate Judiciary Committee Report, Government* Printing Office, 1982

WRIGHT, James D. and ROSSI, Peter, *Armed and Considered Dangerous: A Survey of Felons and Their Firearms (Social Institutions and Social Change),* Aldine de Gruyter, 1994

Index

Symbols

.30-'06 caliber 22, 108
.30-30 caliber 22, 108
.32 ACP 14, 71
.357 magnum ii, 8, 9, 11, 13, 14, 27, 28, 57, 69
.38 Special ii, 13, 14, 39, 68, 69, 71
.380 ACP ii, 14, 68

Numerics

45-degree position 41
7.65 mm 63
9 mm cartridge 61, 63

A

ABC 85, 87
Accidental shootings 21
Addressing the target 45
Air Marshals 49
AK-47 108, 109
Alar scare 90
American Derringer LadyDerringer ii
American Eagle Luger 64
Ant and the Grasshopper, the 86
AR-15 108, 109
Are We There Yet? 49
Aristotle 96, 123
Arming pilots 49
Assault rifles 4
Associated Press 85
Autry, Gene 65
Ayoob, Massad 28

B

Barbra 33
BATF 99
Battle of Lexington, the 95
BBC 49

Beretta model 92F 62
Berkeley, Sir William 95
Bill of Rights v, 3, 4, 50, 75, 79, 80, 83, 92, 96, 101, 102, 104, 126
Billy the Kid 29
Blade position 41
Booth, John Wilkes 70
Borchardt pistol 62
Borchardt, Hugo 62
Bore light 118
Brady, Sarah 91
Branch Davidians 99
Breath control 26, 42, 43
Bullseye shooting 47

C

Callahan, Harry 67
Calling your shots 47
Canted grip 33
Carrying concealed 10
CBS 85, 87
Chamber pressure 13, 54
Charter Arms Bulldog ii, 69, 70, 116
Cleaning a revolver 115
Clinton, Bill 80
Clinton, Hillary 79
Clip 8, 135, 137, 138
CNN 85
Colt Boa ii, 8, 27, 28, 56, 57
Colt Gold Cup Trophy 60, 61
Colt GoldCup pistol 61
Colt Government Model 1991 65
Colt KingCobra 57
Colt model 1911 59, 62
Colt Officer's Model 39, 55
Colt Pony ii, 9, 27, 68
Colt Python 39, 57, 58, 59
Colt Royal Blue 57, 65

0-595-26056-X